If You Can't Say Something Nice

If You Can't Say Something Nice

Calvin Trillin

Ticknor & Fields   New York   1987

Library of Congress Cataloging-in-Publication Data
Trillin, Calvin.
If you can't say something nice.
I. Title.
PS3570.R513   1987   814'.54   87-11259
ISBN 0-89919-531-8
Printed in the United States of America

S 10 9 8 7 6 5 4 3 2 1

The first thirteen pieces in this book first appeared as columns
published in *The Nation*. The remainder were distributed for
publication through King Features Syndicate.

To Jerome Cushman — storyteller,
book-lover, Uncle Jerry

Contents

Contents

If You Can't Say
Something Nice

Introduction

WHEN THE EDITOR of *The Nation*, the wily and parsimonious Victor S. Navasky, said he was going to double the payment for my column, I did the only honorable thing: I resigned.

"I've quit," I told my wife when I got home. "That'll show him to try to double my pay."

"Why didn't you just tell him you got a better offer from the newspaper syndication people?" she said.

"Because I prefer to resign on a matter of principle."

"What, exactly, is the principle involved?"

"Worker solidarity."

"Worker solidarity!" she said. "I never heard you talk about worker solidarity before."

"I never got a better offer before," I said.

"I think it's terrible that all you can talk about, even now that you're leaving *The Nation*, is money," she said.

"That's what the owners of the textile mills in Yorkshire in the nineteenth century used to say about the workers who complained that a family couldn't be supported on two and six a day: 'All they ever talk about is money.'"

The wily and parsimonious Victory S. Navasky hates to talk about money. It makes him break out in hives — at which point he's a dead ringer for a Yorkshire textile-mill owner with chilblains. You'd swear you remember seeing him in one of those gritty North of England movies, being beastly to some decent working man like Tom Courtenay or Alan Bates.

When Navasky and I had lunch in 1978 to discuss his grand vision for transforming *The Nation* from a shabby pinko sheet to a shabby pinko sheet with a humor column and a flashy office for the editor, he didn't even mention money — unless you count the gestures he made as the check arrived and he patted around in his pockets to indicate that he had somehow neglected to bring along any cash. As I reported in the introduction to *Uncivil Liberties*, it was only when I finally asked what he planned to pay for each column that he said, "Something in the high two figures."

For a long time people assumed that "something in the high two figures" was what I was making every three weeks for handing in a column to *The Nation*. I had to point out — in *With All Disrespect*, the sequel to *Uncivil Liberties* — that I had not accepted the high-two-figures offer but had turned the negotiations over to my high-powered agent, Robert (Slowly) Lescher, with instructions to play hardball. Slowly got him up to a hundred. In other words, when the wily and parsimonious Victor S. Navasky offered to double my pay, seven years later, I looked two hundred dollars a column in the face and didn't blink.

"I didn't even blink," I told my wife after the deed was done. "That'll teach him to have the scab security guards throw Albert Finney's crippled little brother down the textile-mill stairs, or whatever he did."

"Don't you feel at all sad about leaving *The Nation*?" my wife said.

"The old W & P will get along without me," I said.

"No doubt," she said. "But will you get along without him? Every time you haven't been able to think of a column idea, you've attacked poor Victor — just the way Ronald Reagan, whenever he was stuck for an answer, used to mention that woman who picked up her Aid for Dependent Children check in a Cadillac."

I hadn't thought of that. Navasky had been, in a manner of speaking, my welfare cheat. Doing the column for newspapers, not only would I have to turn in a piece every week instead of once every three weeks, but I wouldn't have Navasky to kick around anymore. I could imagine the queries that editors of Midwestern dailies would send back to the syndication people if I wrote about the wily and parsimonious Victor S. Navasky: "Who's this Navasky anyway?" or "What's this mean here — 'There's no gonif like a left-wing gonif'?" I suddenly remembered what I had often said in expressing my admiration for the work of my learned colleague Russell Baker, who writes three times a week: "For every column I write, he writes nine, and he doesn't even have Navasky."

I began to have second thoughts. The person who had signed me to the syndication contract — Dennis Allen of the Cowles Syndicate — wore a bow tie and a mustache, and my Uncle Harry had always warned me that the combination of a bow tie and a mustache adds up to flimflam seven times out of ten. Allen had been affable enough when he took Slowly and me to lunch, but why did he keep assuring me that I'd find it easier to write every week than once every three weeks ("Piece of cake, my man, piece of cake")? Why did he keep discussing land opportunities in Florida with the waiter? Was it wise to entrust my future to a man who said he'd make my name a household word in Moline?

Before I could find out — before the column began appearing in newspapers — the Cowles Syndicate was swallowed up by King Features, and the columnists attached to Cowles came along as part of the sale, like furniture in a house that is sold completely furnished. I was an end table.

"Sometimes I feel more like an old sofa," I said to my wife once the column had started. On at least one issue — how much easier it would be to write a weekly column — Allen had justified my Uncle Harry's warning. Here's how hard it is to write a column once a week instead of once every three weeks: three times as hard. I have no way of knowing how the waiter came out in the Florida land deal.

Columnists who are desperate for something to write about cling to the inspiring experience of the aforementioned Baker, who, having stared for hours at a blank piece of paper one afternoon as his deadline approached, finally went for a walk and was almost hit by a potato that had dropped from a high-rise. A column! For some weeks after my weekly deadline had been imposed, I spent a lot of time walking around our neighborhood, waiting for a potato to drop out of a high-rise. We happen to live in Greenwich Village, where there aren't many high-rises. The Village seems to be on the flight path to Kennedy, though, and for a while I nursed the hope that a potato (probably wrapped in foil and filled with sour cream and chives and bacon bits) might fall from a passing 747.

Then my wife said, "Why are you doing this? Russell Baker has already written the falling-potato column anyway." In desperate-moment walks after that, I could only hope for an open manhole cover. If I fell into a manhole and survived, I figured, it was a sure column. If I didn't survive, at least I wouldn't have to write a column.

The president of King Features, Joe D'Angelo, turned out to be a charming man who's nothing at all like a nineteenth-century English mill owner. He's more like the George C. Scott character in *The Hustler* — a smoothie who hunts up newspapers that can be suckered into running my column and then gives me a percentage of the take. The take from each newspaper is about what you'd expect from a neighborhood pool hall the evening before payday. What happens, in a manner of speaking, is that D'Angelo and I walk away together from, say, the *Weehookie Gazette-Tribune* with D'Angelo having already pocketed that week's take — maybe ten dollars. Then he peels a five off his roll, tosses it to me, and says, "Here, kid."

One of the first publications to subscribe to my column was *The Nation*, which was permitted to buy it one week out of three in a special arrangement available only to former exploiters of the author. The payment was the traditional C-note.

"I think it's nice that the column will still be in *The Nation*," my wife said. "And nice that you won't be making fun of Victor Navasky."

"I would never make fun of Navasky," I said. "He's a big payer."

Doing My Talent

December 15, 1984

I CAN WHISTLE and hum at the same time. It's not a trick; it's a talent. If the master of ceremonies at an Elks Club banquet introduced me in the manner sometimes used to introduce Miss America candidates — "Mr. Trillin will now do his talent" — I would whistle and hum at the same time. I would probably whistle and hum "Stars and Stripes Forever," although I've also prepared "Buckle Down, Winsocki" in case of an encore. It's a secure feeling, knowing that you're ready if the Elks call.

I hate to use the phrase "God-given talent" — like a lot of people with God-given talent, I have always prided myself on my lack of pretense — but it's true that whistling and humming at the same time came to me naturally. I didn't work at it, the way I worked at being able to blow a hard-boiled egg out of the shell. It's more like my other talent, the ability to bark like a dog: one day I just realized I could do it.

I can whistle-hum anything, but I'm partial to "Stars and Stripes Forever" because it's a traditional song for people doing my sort of talent. On Ted Mack's *Original Amateur Hour*, a program whose passing I lament, "Stars and Stripes Forever" was a staple. I once saw a man play it on his head with two spoons, varying the notes by how widely he opened his mouth. I suspect he had "Buckle Down, Winsocki" ready as an encore, even though they never did encores on Ted Mack's *Original Amateur Hour*. "Buckle Down Winsocki" is also traditional.

You might think that my ability to whistle and hum at the same time has always been a matter of pride in my family. I know the sort of scenes you're imagining. You see my wife at lunch with one of her friends. "It must be exciting being married to someone who can do a talent," the friend is saying. My wife smiles knowingly. You see my daughters as kindergartners bringing other kids home and begging me to show little Jason and Jennifer and Deirdre how I can whistle and hum at the same time. "Do 'Stars and Stripes Forever,' Daddy," they say. "Then do 'Buckle Down, Winsocki.' " I do both. Even little Jason looks impressed. "Jesus," he says. "I thought I'd seen everything."

That's not the way it has been at all. When my daughters were kindergartners, they never asked me to whistle and hum at the same time for their friends. Little Jason, I know for a fact, still hasn't seen everything, even though he's now sixteen years old. Now that my daughters are teenagers themselves, their response to a bit of spontaneous whistle-humming in a restaurant or an elevator tends to begin with "Daddy, please" — a harbinger, I fear, of the dread "Daddy, this is neither the time nor the place."

I don't know what my wife and her friends say to one another at lunch, but I have to consider the possibility that my wife rolls her eyes up toward the back of her head as her friend asks, "How's the old spoon player these days?" All of this reminds me of what used to be said about the kid in my fourth-grade class who couldn't seem to catch on to math: "He doesn't get much encouragement at home."

Sometimes I find myself yearning for the days when a person could earn respect and maybe even renown for, say, playing the *William Tell* Overture on his teeth. Some of the Big Thinkers out there are probably saying that my nostalgia tells us something about our own times. Big Thinkers believe that most things tell us something about our own times. Here's a Big Thinker interpretation: Once the American people realized that the replacement for what they had dismissed as corny amateur shows was cynical trash like *The Gong Show* or *Real People*, they began to yearn for Ted Mack's *Original Amateur Hour*, and that's what the election of Ronald Reagan was all about. What the voters envisioned when Ronald Reagan mentioned old-fashioned values was Ted Mack presiding over an America where anybody had the freedom to develop the talent to play "Tea for Two" on the Venetian blinds.

Why not? The election of Ronald Reagan had to be all about something, and, as things it might have been all about go, I'd settle for this. I only hope that Reagan acts on the mandate. For instance, public figures should be encouraged to do their talent. I think that a lot of people with God-given talent simply haven't displayed it — perhaps because they don't get much encouragement at home. I like to think the late General Charles de Gaulle could imitate a zither. I like to think Margaret Thatcher can throw a lighted cigarette up in the air and catch it (by the unlit end) in her teeth. I think we'd all be better off if she just went ahead and did it.

I see George Shultz opening up a Cabinet meeting by saying, in his own low-key and sensible way, that he can do a dynamite impression of a whippoorwill at twilight. I see an infectious air of doing your talent running through the meeting — Jim Baker doing his duck calls and Ed Meese imitating a loan shark at bay. Then the President walks over to the window and plays "Tea for Two" on the Venetian blinds.

Sooner or later the Administration could even pressure PBS to bring back Ted Mack's *Original Amateur Hour.* I can see the first show. I'm on it, whistle-humming "Stars and Stripes Forever." They call for an encore. I'm ready.

The Motto-Maker's Art

February 23, 1985

IT WAS INEVITABLE that the controversy over the nomination of Edwin Meese 3d for Attorney General would focus attention on my career as a maker of mottos. I realized that the moment the special prosecutor who was looking into Meese's business dealings with people he later helped appoint to office came up with an endorsement that went something like "Not overtly and obviously and explicitly against the law at the time he did it, at least not in a way anyone could prove." I am widely known in the field, after all, for once having furnished a candidate for mayor of Buffalo with the campaign slogan "Never Been Indicted."

It had never occurred to me that a slogan I composed fifteen or twenty years ago for a municipal election could be used to express the qualifications of a nominee for what is often described as the nation's highest legal office, but, as they used to say in Buffalo, a good slogan will stretch to two or three campaigns. And once it became obvious that "Never Been Indicted" was the appropriate motto for the Meese forces, it was natural for people to poke around in my *œuvre* to see if they could find other examples of the perspicacious pithiness so prized among motto-makers. (As it happens, the motto of the American Association of Motto-Makers is "Perspicacious Pithiness Prized.")

It occurred to me, of course, that the attention brought by the Meese nomination might be a good opportunity to set up shop professionally. "Strike while the iron is hot!" I said to my wife — quoting, as it happens, a motto I suggested to the International Brotherhood of Pants Pressers during some labor strife in the garment trade. She didn't say anything, although she seemed to be looking at me with the same expression she wore last year when I asked her if she thought it was too late for me to switch careers and try my luck as a cabaret singer.

Her lack of enthusiasm might have come from memories of a fallow period I went through as a motto-maker, when I seemed to be devoting most of my energy to criticizing the mottos of others. I wrote to *Forbes* magazine, for instance, to say that its motto, "Capitalist Tool," sounded like something a Russian premier might shout at an American president over the hot line in a moment of complete exasperation — as in "You've wiped out Rumania by mistake, you capitalist tool!" I knew that some of my colleagues were beginning to say that my work was flawed by a certain negativism — that I had lost the positive punch I had years ago when I invented what became a renowned motto for our family: "Zip Up Your Jacket." It got so I wasn't doing much new work except for sending unsolicited proposals for fresh mottos to some American cities, just to keep my hand in. What hurt most was that the folks in Minneapolis ("Home of the Late April Slush") and Akron ("Preferable to Youngstown") did not even trouble to respond.

The lesson of Edwin Meese's appointment, it seemed to me, was that I had been aiming too low in those days. I should have been composing at the state level at the very least. If I had any doubt about the need of many states for a professional hand at motto-making, it evaporated when, shortly after the Meese hearings, I saw a new license plate from Pennsylvania. Where the motto "Keystone State" had been, the license plate read "You've Got a Friend in Pennsylvania." Is that what people in Pennsylvania think of as perspicacious pithiness? The old "Keystone State" motto was to my mind a very professional piece of work. It conjured up a monument in downtown Philadelphia made of pure keystone, and the great forges of Pittsburgh turning out one keystone after another, and in the Amish farmland lovely fields of keystones rippling in the breeze. Then I realized that many states had no motto at all, not even some lame footshuffler like "Oklahoma Is OK." I started sketching out a new business card.

"There's an opening here for the right person," I said to my wife.

"Particularly if his voice doesn't crack on the high notes," she said, with a sarcasm I thought completely out of place in a discussion of career choices.

I had already worked out a motto for the Nebraska license plate: "A Long Way Across." Arkansas presented a problem. My first effort, "Not As Bad As You Might Imagine," seemed a bit verbose, but I was certain I could edit it down to something pithy — maybe something in the Oklahoma mold, like "Not So Bad." I already had an admirably pithy one for Florida: "Condo Heaven."

After a while, national administrations would come to call. The Reagan people, conscious that neither "The New Federalism" nor "A New Beginning" had caught on, might ask me to come up with some new New. It occurred to me that I should prepare a memorandum on the motto implications of Reagan's State of the Union message. I would counsel against pushing that phrase "A Second American Revolution": any reminder of the first American Revolution could drive some rich opponents of Reagan's flat-tax plan to toss their machine tools into Los Angeles harbor while chanting "No Taxation Without Depreciation." I'd suggest something short and snappy for the second-term motto — maybe "Voodoo II."

"What qualifications do you have to advise the President?" my wife asked when I told her of my expectations.

I held up my new business card. Under my name it said "Never Been Indicted."

Iran May Be Iraq

March 16, 1985

THE PERSON at the office we call Harold the Committed suspects that I'm not keeping myself informed on the war between Iran and Iraq. He's right. Keeping yourself informed on a war has something in common with watching a football game on television: it's not much fun if you don't care who wins. If you'd just as soon see both sides lose, it's no fun at all. A pacifist friend of mine used to grow gloomy every year on the weekend of the Army-Navy football game. When we'd ask what was troubling him, he would always say, "About all you can hope for is that one side or the other suffers a defeat of humiliating proportions."

Harold the Committed suspects that I sometimes skip the entire Sunday edition of the *New York Times*. He's wrong about that. I'll admit that I don't read the *Times* as thoroughly as Harold does. He has imposed on himself a very strict regimen for getting through the entire paper on Sunday. He begins sharply at nine, and he is allowed only one half-hour break before lunch — to watch *Face the Nation.* The rules about finishing are strict: if he hasn't completed every section except Travel and Real Estate by two, he's required to read the editorials all over again.

I concentrate on the wedding announcements myself. From reading about the background of the bride and groom, I try to imagine what sort of tension there will be at the reception. Last Sunday, for instance, when I read about the nuptials of Hatcher Thatcher Baxter 3d, almost all of whose ancestors signed the Declaration of Independence, and Mary Catherine Garrity, whose father, Timothy, was described in a way that led me to believe he is a subway motorman, I couldn't help but wonder whether Tim Garrity would feel the need to knock back a few with the boys before finally facing the sort of people he thought he had raised his daughter to despise, and if so, what effect that would have on the wedding toasts.

That doesn't leave me much time for the war between Iran and Iraq, but I'm not the only one not keeping himself informed on that war. I'm convinced that a lot of people get Iran and Iraq mixed up, so they don't know who to root for. It's as if both teams were wearing red jerseys. Also, a lot of people who actually can tell Iran and Iraq apart suspect that they're fighting simply because they've both been driven around the bend by having been mixed up with each other all these years.

Iran and Iraq must blame each other for the confusion. How would you feel if you decided to change your name from Mesopotamia to Iraq for the usual reasons — it fits better in headlines, it sounds less foreign — and then a country right next door that has a perfectly good name of its own, Persia, started calling itself Iran? How would you like it, on the other hand, if you changed your name to Iran for absolutely appropriate reasons — your country happens to be on the Iran River, one of the world's great salmon- and trout-fishing streams — only to find out that an obscure country right next door has started calling itself Iraq for no earthly reason (since "iraq" is the Arabic word for door hinge)? It would be embarrassing for either one of them to change back, so about the only thing to do is to have a war.

I think I would be keeping myself better informed on it if I thought it was a war that Denmark had any chance at all of winning. I root for Denmark. If you know anything bad about Denmark, I don't want to hear it. I've never been to Denmark myself, and I avoid stories about it in the Sunday *Times*. I'm afraid I might find out that Denmark persecutes a Finnish minority or underpays its goalie or something, and then I'd be left with no one to root for. Except, of course, the United States of America — my home team. I was a strong rooter for the USA in World War II. I kept myself very well informed on that war, even though I was only a child. My father had told me that when the USA won that war we'd have bubble gum again. You might say I had a stake in that war. Also, as soon as the USA won that war I could quit collecting newspapers for General Eisenhower. I hated collecting newspapers for General Eisenhower. I couldn't imagine what he wanted with that many copies of the *Kansas City Star*. After a while, I began to envision General Eisenhower sitting over in Europe somewhere behind a sort of fortress of newspapers, chewing bubble gum.

Of course, I've kept myself informed on some wars I didn't have a stake in. Several years ago I got very interested in the war between Yemen and South Yemen. What intrigued me was that as far as I could tell from the maps of the battlefront, South Yemen is not south of Yemen — except for a tiny smidgen, like the tiny smidgen of Missouri that is east of Arkansas. South Yemen is mostly east of Yemen, except for some of it that's actually a little bit north. Also, South Yemen happens to be a lot bigger than Yemen, so by rights it should have been called Yemen and the other place should have been called West Yemen or maybe even South Yemen.

That, I told Harold, was obviously the reason for the war. "I'm from Missouri, Hal the C," I said, "and I can tell you that if everyone started referring to Missouri as East Arkansas, we'd fight." Harold shook his head and said the point of the war was which Yemen was a "Soviet client" and which was an "American client." When Harold talks like that, he can make a perfectly good war sound like a brawl in the waiting room of a claims lawyer.

Apparently, the *Times* carried another of those stories about clients last Sunday — or maybe another report on the war between Mesopotamia and Persia — because at the office the next day Harold the Committed asked me if I had ready the Sunday *Times* carefully.

"You bet, Hal the C," I said.

"Well, what do you think?" he said.

"I think Garrity's going to get up and tell the Baxters that he hasn't met such a bunch of stiffs since he visited Madame Tussaud's Wax Museum the time he went to London on the Knights of Columbus tour," I said. In the wedding announcement section, I usually know who to root for.

The Line on Lines

February 2, 1985

I BEGAN my study of Manhattan crosstown bus-boarding customs with confidence that it would put to rest once and for all the question of whether I am a serious researcher or simply a crank. From the moment I observed a line of people waiting at the crosstown bus stop on East Seventy-ninth and York early one Wednesday morning, I realized that I was onto something big. I was certain that there were no reports of Manhattan bus lines in the literature; I keep up with the journals. Orderly lines of any sort are so rare in New York that I can recall only one scholarly article on the subject in the past decade — a study of what sandwich makers at Katz's Delicatessen, on the Lower East Side, say to customers who push ahead (see " 'Whadaya, Lady, a Movie Star?': A Study of Anglo-Yiddish Pejorative Vernacular," *Journal of Linear Studies*, June 1979).

My own fieldwork has been done mainly in Europe, where I spent several years studying degrees of ovalness in Italian lines; I later published the seminal study establishing that French lines are triangular in shape, with the base of the triangle at the place where business is being conducted (see "Point Man to the Rear: Cartesian Triangularity in Modern France," *The Queue Review*, Spring 1968).

I don't know how the crank talk got started, but I suspect it had something to do with the incident in London. Ironically, this was during a period of remarkable productivity for me — when I made the breakthrough discovery that a lot of English people line up for fun. I can still remember the moment I realized what I was onto: it was a bright spring evening, and the family I was observing, the Tootingbecs, had been in four sweets queues without having bought a thing.

"Lovely, isn't it," Maurice Tootingbec said to his children as they all dropped out of the fourth sweets queue just before reaching the counter. "Let's go queue for the Number 31 bus for a while and then walk home."

There was no reason for me to be surprised, then, when I turned into a doorway on New Bond Street to light a cigarette and a queue of thirty-five English people formed behind me. Yes, I'll admit that I found it a bit irritating when they proceeded to follow me down the street; we all know how important it is for the observer to remain detached from what he is observing. "I was just lighting a cigarette," I finally said to the man behind me.

"Thanks awfully, but I gave it up," he said. "But thanks very much indeed."

Yes, after twenty minutes of this, I might have raised my voice. Yes, one of the things I said might have been, "I won't be followed by overpolite foreigners!" Yes, I did dash across Oxford Street just as the light was turning red. But if that was a move dictated by temper rather than by scientific inquiry, as those who spread the crank talk would have us believe, how does one explain the scholarly article it produced — "How Stiff the Upper Lip: British Queue Discipline under Stress in the West End of London" (*Lineup: A Canadian Journal of Waiting*, Fall 1962)?

I knew I had to be thorough — that is, I had to observe crosstown bus-boarding customs on the West Side as well as on the East Side. I went to Seventy-ninth and Broadway and found my thoroughness rewarded. The people waiting for the crosstown bus there were not in line. In fact, when the doors of the bus opened, the crowd trying to climb aboard was so unruly that I was knocked to the pavement by a man who had lunged suddenly to crowd in front of a pregnant woman. Fieldwork is not without risks. How well we all remember Ralph W. Bermondsey, the lottery-line specialist who became preoccupied while observing a queue in Punta del Este in 1948 and discovered too late that he had enlisted in the Uruguayan merchant marine.

Lines on the East Side but no lines on the West Side! For a serious researcher, that raised intriguing questions. Was there a correlation between the number of stockbrokers living on the East Side and the presence of lines? If so, why is the floor of the Stock Exchange so much like a West Side bus stop? Had a lot more people on the East Side been to England? Had a lot more people on the West Side been to Italy? (See " 'Marone!': Patterns of Injury among Neapolitans Attempting to Board Rush-Hour Buses," *Journal of Orderly Procession*, February 1974.) The risk of being trampled on the West Side would not be the only difficulty in gathering data. From preliminary observations, I realized that an interviewer would have trouble getting the East Side line-standers to turn their attention from a close perusal of the *Wall Street Journal*.

And would I find it just a bit irritating that in New York, the home of the push and the shove, people were lining up for buses? Was it troubling that most of those so lined looked like those maddeningly organized twenty-six-year-old MBAs who make $65,000 a year and jog every morning from six to six forty-five and switch their money from copra futures to limited partnership real estate deals while I'm watching *Mary Tyler Moore Show* reruns?

"I'm a researcher, not a crank," I said as I approached an East Side line of forty or so carefully turned-out young professionals. I realized that I had spoken aloud, but nobody looked up from the *Wall Street Journal*. I happened to glance across Seventy-ninth Street: there was the crosstown bus line. Then what line was this? Just then, a taxi stopped, the first person in line climbed in, and everyone else took one step forward. A taxi line! In a town where battling for a taxi has been raised to the level of a revered martial art, these people were standing in a taxi line, like a bunch of overpolite foreigners. Yes, I might have raised my voice. Yes, one of the things I said might have been, "You're ruining this city, you repressed little creeps!" What my detractors don't understand, though, is that this was all for research. I'm working on the article now — "Yuppies Provoked: Attempts to Distract from the *Wall Street Journal* the Sort of People Who Would Form a Taxi Line in Manhattan." It will be in the Spring issue of *Crank Quarterly*.

Fred's Fiftieth

WHEN FRED'S fiftieth birthday came around, I decided to give him an American Polled Hereford Association T-shirt. They're awfully nice. It was a difficult decision. Finding Fred a birthday gift used to be a snap. Fred has always been a pretty good beer drinker, and he travels around the country a lot; at some point, his friends put those two facts together and decided that what he would want for his birthday was some obscure American beer. It was similar to what might be decided about a hard-to-please uncle who once expressed a mild interest in elephants and now knows that every birthday will bring more statues and drawings and models of elephants, an animal he long ago came to hate.

The problem was not that Fred had come to hate beer. Fred's got a serious tolerance for beer. The problem was that regional American foodstuffs had become fashionable: it had got so that there no longer was such a thing as an obscure American beer. When trendy joints in SoHo — places that cater to the sort of people who spend a lot of time deciding what brand of sneakers to buy — started serving only, say, Rolling Rock and Genesee, it was obvious that you could no longer walk into Fred's birthday party with a six-pack of Grain Belt and expect to get a big hello.

Fred doesn't raise Polled Herefords — he doesn't really have the acreage for that sort of operation where he lives now, in Brooklyn — but, as I said, the American Polled Hereford Association T-shirt is awfully nice. It has an abstract cow on the front. You wouldn't think the Polled Hereford people would go for an abstract cow, but the Polled Hereford people can fool you.

The writing above and below the abstract cow says POLLED HEREFORDS — AN AMERICAN IDEA SINCE 1901. That happens to be my favorite Polled Hereford motto. The Polled Hereford people have more than one. For instance, it says THE TREND IS TO POLLED HEREFORDS on the mechanical pencil, which has a tiny cow floating in liquid where most pencils have erasers. The sweatshirt says POLLED HEREFORDS — THE BIG, BOLD BREED, and so does the baseball cap. For a while, I thought about giving Fred both a Polled Hereford T-shirt and a Polled Hereford baseball cap — it's what I think the fashion people call an ensemble — but finally I announced to my wife, "I've decided that the T-shirt ought to do it. The American Polled Hereford Association T-shirts are awfully nice."

"What happened to the idea of giving him both the T-shirt and the baseball cap?" she asked.

"It wouldn't be right to give him an ensemble with clashing mottos," I said. "Fred's an old friend, and I'd hate to see him embarrass himself."

"Are you sure you aren't just being selfish?"

"Selfish!" I said. "How can you use that word to someone who's handed over as much Grain Belt beer to Fred as

I have? Also someone, I might just mention, who considered giving Fred an entire box of bourbon-filled chocolates from Kentucky *in addition to* the American Polled Hereford Association T-shirt."

I had received the chocolates as a gift myself. The person who gave them to me said they were illegal in all but three states, presumably because of the bourbon. We are talking, in other words, about a product that the authorities take seriously.

"Why aren't you giving him the chocolates?" my wife asked.

"My mother told me it's rude to give away a gift," I said. "Also, how are we to know if this is one of the legal states?"

"If you were a truly generous person, you'd give Fred a few pieces of that Cajun boudin you've got in the freezer," my wife said.

My boudin! Before going any further, I'd like to say a few things about the Cajun version of boudin. The first thing is that it's just about my favorite food; the second thing is that it's impossible to come by outside of South Louisiana; and the third thing is that I wasn't about to give so much as a tiny morsel of it to Fred. Our friend James had brought the boudin from New Iberia, Louisiana. I might just mention, considering the ugly insinuations I've been obligated to record here concerning my standards of generosity, that in appreciation I presented him with my last copy of *The Woman's Day Book of Gelatin Cookery*.

"What about what my mother said about giving away a gift?" I asked.

"After all the hinting you did to get that boudin, it was less a gift than a takeout order," she said.

I saw nothing untoward about giving a little encouragement. James, after all, had to do research throughout South Louisiana to make certain he was bringing the best boudin. His was an extraordinary effort — requiring, I suspect, the consumption of hundreds of pounds of boudin, not to mention the trouble involved in hauling the final selection all the way to New York in an ice chest approximately the size of a Honda Civic.

"After all the trouble James went to, I can't imagine that you'd want me to hand out that boudin to any slight acquaintance I happened to run into," I said.

"Slight acquaintance! You and Fred have been friends for at least twenty years."

"He's a hard person to know," I said. "Also, I'm giving him practically my only American Polled Hereford Association T-shirt as it is."

"It *is* your only American Polled Hereford Association T-shirt," she said. "I threw away the one with the rip and the permanent boudin stain."

I hadn't realized that. I love American Polled Hereford Association T-shirts. They're awfully nice. I walked straight to the refrigerator. "Do you know what Fred might like for his fiftieth, just for old times' sake?" I said as I started rummaging around in the back of the bottom shelf. "A six-pack of Grain Belt."

Catawba and Château Lafite-Rothschild taste rather Jewish. Also, he has admitted to me that when blindfolded even wine experts cannot usually tell red wine from white wine. This is astonishing but absolutely true. Check it out. Yes, I do occasionally write something that is absolutely true. It's one of my hidden facets.

During my recent trip to the Napa Valley, Bruce and I met for a drink, and he said he needed some wine advice. I figured Bruce needed the sort of guidance that can sometimes be provided by people who have a natural instinct for connoisseurship — say, whether pinot noir would be appropriate with hog jowls. Yes, if you must know, I was a bit flattered.

What he needed, Bruce said, was some help figuring out how to make his wine attractive to people who know so little about wine that they choose it according to the name or the label design or the price or, in extreme cases, the shape of the bottle. I looked around the bar. We were the only ones there.

"For instance," Bruce said, "what sort of scene do you like on the label?"

I thought it over for a few moments. I finally concluded that what Bruce wanted was, in fact, simply a type of wine consultation. But you must have known that all along.

"A mountain," I said. "I like a nice mountain."

At that moment the waitress showed up to take our order.

"I'll have a glass of red wine," Bruce said. "Unless you feel like bringing white."

"J&B on the rocks for me," I said. "With a twist."

My Life in Wine

April 27, 1985

I THINK IT WOULD BE FAIR to say that I was in the Napa Valley recently as a wine consultant. Yes, I'm aware that you didn't realize I know anything about wine. You have been under the impression that when it comes to my feeding habits I might be just a tiny bit unsophisticated. Don't be afraid to say so. I know what you're thinking: you don't understand how someone whose name has any number of times been used in the same sentence with phrases like "pigging out" could be a wine consultant in the Napa Valley. Maybe the reason you don't understand is that you don't know precisely what a wine consultant in the Napa Valley does. After all, you have never been one yourself. I thought I'd just mention that.

Yes, I did rather enjoy eating in the San Francisco Bay Area while I was out there. What was that? Too sophisticated? No, I did not find the New California Cuisine too sophisticated. Yes, I'll admit that I was relieved to find that there were still some pigeons left in the squares of San Francisco; it had occurred to me that since my previous visit, every last one of them might have been snatched up, smoked, and thrown on a bed of radicchio. Yes, it is true that I once expressed some concern about the amount of goat cheese being served in the Bay Area, but that was before I learned that you don't have to kill a goat to get the cheese. I like the New California Cuisine. I like California wine, too. I think it has integrity. Plenty of integrity.

No, this is not some sort of mistake. Yes, I know you had associated me more with soda pop, or maybe beer. Domestic beer. It just goes to show you. People have hidden facets. Here's one of my hidden facets: I don't know much about soda pop. It was only five or six years ago that I acquired (from a San Francisco radio talk-show host named Jim Eason) the basic drill on which soft drink goes with which sort of food. It's Coke or Royal Crown with meat, 7-Up or ginger ale with fish, and Dr. Pepper with game. But you must have known that all along. Even though I didn't, I must say I spent a lot of my childhood eating hamburgers washed down with cherry Cokes — precisely the proper combination. When it comes to connoisseurship, I suppose there must be such a thing as a natural instinct.

Still, I don't make any claims about being an authority on soda pop. My daughter came home from school one day recently with the announcement that Coke and 7-Up were impossible to tell apart if you tasted them while blindfolded and holding your nose. I suppose someone who is sure of his ground on soda pop questions might have said, "Ten bucks says you're wrong, buster," or something like that. I didn't. I was willing to give it a try. What she hadn't said was that it isn't easy to drink Coke or 7-Up

while holding your nose, unless you're the sort of person who approaches nose-holding from above. Being blindfolded didn't help either. But I gave it a try, and, as happens, I was able to tell Coke from 7-Up. I don't claim to know much about soda pop, but aftertaste I know.

I don't know much about beer, either. That's another one of my hidden facets. Yes, I know I've been in a number of late-night conversations with the sort of drinkers whose pedantry about beer increases with their consumption of it. But I don't say much in those conversations. If someone asks me whether I like a particular beer, I say yes. It's true; I like them all. I feel the same way about beer that I feel about ocean views: I'm always happy to have one, but I wouldn't want to put any money on my ability to distinguish among them.

Actually, I don't think many beer pedants can tell one beer from another, any more than those traveling salesmen who think they're impressing the cocktail waitress by saying "J&B on the rocks with a twist" could tell J&B from the sort of Scotch served at faculty cocktail parties. I don't think it would even be necessary to require them to hold their noses during the test, although I'll admit that a roomful of blindfolded traveling salesmen drinking J&B on the rocks while holding their noses might make a pretty sight.

I was asked to be a consultant by my friend Bruce, who makes wine in the Napa Valley. For someone who works in the wine trade, Bruce is quite open-minded. Unlike some other Napa wine people I met on a previous visit, he had not dismissed out of hand my observation, made during a discussion about similarities in certain American and French wines, that both Manischewitz Cream

Still Truly Needy

May 18, 1985

A LOT OF PEOPLE wish I wouldn't carry on so about the plight of Philip Caldwell. I know that. I've known that for some time. I can see people edging away from me at parties, the way they edge away from Harold the Committed when he's on one of his toots about saving the whales. I realize my friends discuss what can be done about my "Caldwell thing." Some of them have approached me about it, in a kindly way. "Give it a rest," they say. "Let it go."

They say that they really respected me for taking up the cause of Philip Caldwell in 1980 — the year he didn't get any incentive bonus at all, even though it was perfectly obvious that he was giving it everything he had — but that it's time to move on to something else. That's what they say now; that's not the way I remember it. The way I remember it, they told me even then that the president of the Ford Motor Company was not an appropriate subject for my sympathy. They scoffed at my notion that Philip Caldwell was the sort of person the Reagan Administration had in mind in its pronouncements about looking after the "truly needy." They reminded me that even without an incentive bonus Philip Caldwell was making $400,000 a year. I said that it didn't make any difference how much money you made if your kid came home from school every day in tears because all the other kids had thrown spark plugs and hood ornaments at him while chanting, "Your old man's got no incentive."

"O.K., maybe he really was what they meant by 'truly needy' then," my friend Max said to me the other night at the Milledges' anniversary party as he joined me in the corner, where, I'll admit, I was standing quite alone. "But I just read in *Business Week* that last year he made more than four million. That must be what Reagan means by people being able to pull themselves up by their own bootstraps. He's O.K. So listen, now that Reagan has said that the *contras* are the moral equivalent of the Founding Fathers, which one do you think is the most like Benjamin Franklin?"

Good old Max. I could see what he was trying to do. He was trying to get me interested in the issues of the day so that I'd talk about something other than Philip Caldwell and wouldn't have to stand alone in the corner at parties. As it happens, I know which *contra* is the most like Benjamin Franklin. It's Colonel Rafael (Hot Stuff) Rodriguez, who used to be in charge of the Bureau of Persuasive Interrogation for Somoza's National Guard. Hot Stuff shares with Ben Franklin a keen interest in the practical applications of the phenomenon of electricity.

But that wasn't the sort of thing I wanted to talk about, considering what has happened lately to poor Phil Caldwell. The way I see it, Caldwell is in worse shape than ever. In 1980, when all of the other guys at the club sort of smiled in his direction as they discussed their incentive bonuses, he could at least feel superior to Lee Iacocca. In fact, I pointed out at the time that under a system of disincentive nega-bonuses I had proposed for American executives, Caldwell, who had managed to lose the company $1.5 billion that year, would have owed Ford $274,358; Iacocca would have owed Chrysler Ford.

So Phil Caldwell, clawing and scratching in the American way, finally pulls himself up to $4 million a year, and what does he find? Lee Iacocca. Lee Iacocca on television. Lee Iacocca on the cover of *Time*. Lee Iacocca listed right there on the cover of *Business Week* as someone who makes $1 million a year more from Chrysler than Philip Caldwell makes from Ford. Lee Iacocca's book has been number one on the best-seller list for six months. Lee Iacocca is commonly referred to as a folk hero. Lee Iacocca has drinks with Frank Sinatra at the "21" Club. Lee Iacocca is engaged to a former airline stewardess. How do you think it makes Phil Caldwell feel to pull himself up by his own bootstraps, nearly fracturing his tibia in the process, and then find all that? I'll tell you how: like fate has given him five in the mush.

Before I could tell Max in detail about these lamentable developments, we were joined by Jake, another old friend, who asked me how I thought the White House advance men had managed to get Reagan scheduled for a visit to a German military cemetery that has Waffen S.S. troops buried in it. Good old Jake. I'd bet that just before Max and Jake left for the Milledges' they had a little caucus on the telephone to figure out the best topics for distracting me from what I know they consider an obsession with the plight of Phil Caldwell. They do have my best interests at heart. They're my pals.

And, by chance, I know exactly how the White House people got Reagan into such an embarrassing pickle. Nobody else seems to remember that it was during a trip to Germany late in February to do the advance work for this very presidential visit that Michael Deaver, the White House Deputy Chief of Flacks, used his temporary diplomatic passport to buy a BMW at the special discount price available to diplomats — an incident that bolstered the belief of some political observers that the familial little group of people who have been clustered around Ronald Reagan since his days in Sacramento should be referred to as the nuclear sleaze. During the entire trip, the junior advance men must have kept asking Deaver if he was sure it wasn't necessary to find out who was buried at Bitburg.

"Mmmm," Deaver would say as he slowly turned the pages of his BMW catalogue. "Do you think I can get along without the voice-activated windshield wipers or not? You'd think they'd throw that sort of thing in free for a diplomat."

But that's not what I wanted to spend my time discussing. Not after what had happened to Phil Caldwell. "Listen, Jake," I said. "How would you like it if some guy you used to refer to as Old Pasta Gut had the number-one best seller and you'd had eight publishers turn down your collected annual addresses to the Mercury dealers? Just how would you feel, Jake? Jake?"

Jake was backing toward the middle of the room. "I think I'll just freshen up this drink," he said.

I turned to Max, but Max was edging away.

Whom Says So?

June 8, 1985

COMES NOW A LETTER from a reader I'll call W. E. (Ned) Chilton III, of Charleston, West Virginia, who has some criticism of my grammar. That's flashy syntax, by the way — that "comes now" business. I'm using it in this instance partly to show off — you'd be surprised how many people don't think I know any flashy syntax — and partly in the hope that its flashiness will tend to obscure a slight lack of candor. The letter from Chilton III didn't just comes now; it cames a couple of months ago. I haven't answered it yet — and not, I hasten to say, because its point is so well taken that it leaves no room for reply. On the grammar question, Chilton III happens to be wrong. I would simply write him that and be done with it, but I'm afraid that if I answer Chilton III's letter he'll answer my answer. Chilton III obviously has a secretary; his secretary obviously has a word processor. I'd never be able to keep up. Correspondence can be like a war between two countries of unequal industrial might: it's helpful to have God on your side, but you can still be outgunned.

There are a lot of ways wars can end — a truce, a sur-
render, the complete destruction of the planet — but
there's no established way to end a correspondence. I'm
not talking now about trying to get the last word in a
contentious correspondence — a correspondence, say,
that begins when one person, in an appalling display of
nit-picking, criticizes another person's grammar, and that
person, in a noble and dignified way, tells the first person
to stick it in his ear. I'm talking about a perfectly friendly
correspondence. If, for instance, Joe writes Harvey a note
telling him that he enjoyed Harvey's remarks at the
kickoff banquet of the Irish Bar and Luau Division of the
Bonds for Israel Drive, Harvey is likely to write back a
thank-you note that goes on to say that the generosity
of Joe's pledge made clear his understanding of the essential point of the speech — that people who own or manage
Irish bars have a special responsibility for the Holy Land.
Which means that Joe has to write Harvey back, thanking
him for the compliment about the generosity of his pledge.
Does that letter have to be answered by Harvey? There is
no mechanism that permits a U.N. peacekeeping team,
using troops from Canada and Denmark, to step in and
administer a negotiated cease-fire.

Years ago I tried to take care of such problems by writing my congressman to ask that he introduce what I
called Truce in Answering legislation. Under my law, Joe
could have simply added at the end of his first letter, in
the lower left-hand corner, "RNA." That would mean
Reply Not Anticipated. It wouldn't mean that Joe would
refuse to read a reply from Harvey. It would simply
mean that Joe, having said what he had to say, was willing to cool it. If Harvey didn't feel the need to carry on

this little exchange, he wouldn't have to worry about the possibility that Joe would go around town saying, "Now Harvey thinks he's such a big shot he doesn't have to answer his mail, but I knew him when he was schlepping dirty dishes at Sidney's Shillelagh." I'm using the conditional tense here not just because it's a flashy tense. The legislation was not passed. My congressman never answered my letter.

If Chilton III is reading this, he is beginning to think that all of the talk about my RNA campaign might be a diversion that reflects an unwillingness to confront the issue he raised in criticizing my grammar. Wrong again, Chilton III; that's twice in a row. I'm eager to confront the issue because it goes to the heart of another one of my campaigns — an effort to purge the language of the word "whom." The sentence Chilton III pounced on was the following: "I usually know who to root for." Chilton III thought I should have said, "I usually know whom to root for." He's wrong, of course. If I ever used the word "whom," he might have had a point, but I never use the word "whom." I gave it up completely. That's part of my campaign.

As far as I'm concerned, "whom" is a word that was invented to make everyone sound like a butler. Nobody who is not a butler has ever said it out loud without feeling just a little bit weird. Any number of great quotations would have been lost to history if the speaker had shown the bad judgment to employ the word "whom." Take the memorable response made by Ross Barnett, a governor of Mississippi in the early 1960s, when he was questioned about a prison trusty who had failed to return from an out-of-state trip that some people thought he shouldn't have been allowed to make in the first place: "If you can't trust a trusty, who can you trust?"

I know what you're thinking. You're thinking that Chilton III, had he been in Ross Barnett's shoes, might have said, "If one cannot trust one's trusty, whom can one trust?" You're thinking that Chilton III might be a butler. You're thinking that what Chilton III really thought I should have said in the sentence he criticized was, "I usually know for whom to root." You're thinking that Chilton III is the sort of person who, when standing in a bar that caters to tough types who put a lot of money on sporting events, might turn to the bozo next to him and say, "Whom do you like in the Series?"

I think you're being too hard on Chilton III. He just wants to be correct. What he doesn't realize is this: if a lot of people quit using "whom," pretty soon nobody will have to use it. That's how the campaign works! After a while, the people who preside over such matters will simply decide that, usage having changed, "who" is always acceptable; they'll use the change as an occasion for writing little essays about how language is a living thing. It won't take long. Look how quickly they caved in on "hopefully."

I really should write a letter to Chilton III telling him all this, as soon as I can get around to it. "We'll all be free, Chilton III," I'll say. "Without fear of breaking any rules of grammar, you'll be able to put down a few dollars on the Series without having some bozo say, 'Whadaya, a weirdo or something?'" In the lower left-hand corner of the letter I'll write "RNA."

Old Marrieds

August 3, 1985

I FIGURED the big question about our twentieth wedding anniversary might be whether the local newspaper would send a reporter out to interview us, the way reporters always used to interview those old codgers who managed to hit one hundred. ("Mr. Scroggins offers no formula for longevity, although he acknowledged that he has polished off a quart of Jim Beam whiskey every day of his adult life.") I figured that might be the big question even though the local newspaper is the *Village Voice*. Or maybe I figured that might be the big question *because* the local newspaper is the *Village Voice*. In Greenwich Village, after all, we are known rather widely for being married. We enjoy a mild collateral renown for having children. Several years ago, in fact, I expressed concern that we might be put on the Gray Line tour of Greenwich Village as a nuclear family.

It occurred to me that all this might be vaguely embarrassing; in recent years it has become common to hear people all over the country speak of long-term marriage

in a tone of voice that assumes it to be inextricably intertwined with the music of Lawrence Welk. In the presence
of someone who has been married a long time to the
same person, a lot of people seem to feel the way they
might feel in the presence of a Methodist clergyman or
an IRS examiner. When I asked a friend of mine recently
how his twenty-fifth college reunion had gone — he had
attended with the very same attractive and pleasant
woman he married shortly after graduation — he said,
"Well, after the first day I decided to start introducing
Marge as my second wife, and that seemed to make
everyone a lot more comfortable."

This awkwardness in the presence of marriage has, of
course, been particularly intense in the Village, a neighborhood so hip that it is no longer unusual to see people
wearing their entire supply of earrings on one ear. (" 'I
don't hold with jewelry or none of them geegaws,' Mr.
Scroggins said, 'although over the long haul I've found
that a single gold stud in one ear can set off a spring
ensemble to good advantage.' ") In the Village, a lot of
people don't get married, and a lot of those who do seem
to get unmarried pretty much on the way back from the
ceremony. In other words, the institution has been leak-
ing from both ends.

When our older daughter was in first grade at P.S. 3,
one of the romantically named grade schools in the
Village, I happened to be among the parents escorting the
class on a lizard-buying expedition to a local purveyor
called Exotic Aquatics. As we crossed Seventh Avenue,
the little boy I had by the hand looked up at me and said,
"Are you divorced yet?" When I said that I wasn't, he
didn't make fun of me or anything like that — they teach
tolerance at P.S. 3, along with a smattering of spelling —

but I could sense his discomfort in having to cross a major artery in the company of someone who was a little bit behind.

Reaching a twentieth anniversary might just increase such discomfort among our neighbors. I could imagine what would be said if that little boy's parents happened to meet by chance now and our names came up. (As I envision the sort of lives they lead, she has just quit living with her psychotherapist in New Jersey to join a radical feminist woodcutting collective; her former husband is in the process of breaking up with a waitress who has decided that what she really wants to do is direct.) "Oh, them!" the woodcutter would say. "Why, they've been married for *decades!*"

The more I considered it, the more I thought that if a reporter in our neighborhood came out to interview people on the twentieth anniversary of their marriage, the questions might be less like the ones he'd ask a citizen who had reached the age of one hundred than the ones he'd ask someone who has chosen to construct a replica of the 1939 World's Fair out of multicolored toothpicks in his recreation room. ("Tell me, Mr. McVeeter, is this some sort of nutso fixation, or what?")

Then I happened to run into an old college classmate called Martin G. Kashfleau. In both investments and social trends, Kashfleau prides himself on having just got out of what other people are about to get into and having just got in on the ground floor of what other people haven't yet heard about. After Kashfleau filled me in on his recent activities — he had just got out of whelk-farming tax shelters and into chewing of hallucinogenic kudzu — he asked what I'd been up to.

"Twentieth anniversary," I mumbled.

"Terrific!" Kashfleau said. He looked at me as if I had just revealed that I was in on the ground floor of a hot electronics issue. At least, I think that's the way he looked at me; I really don't have much experience at being looked at as if I had just revealed that I was in on the ground floor of a hot electronics issue.

Kashfleau told me that among people in their twenties marriage has come back into fashion. As he explained the way things have been going, marriage is part of a sort of fifties revival package that includes neckties and naked ambition. "Best thing you ever did," Kashfleau said. "They're all doing it now, but look at the equity you've got built up."

I shrugged modestly. You don't brag about that sort of thing. Then I went home and told my wife that we were in fashion.

"Not while you're wearing that jacket we're not," she said.

I told her about the fifties package that people in their twenties were bringing back into vogue. She said that if the alternative was to be identified with those little strivers, she would prefer to be thought of as inextricably intertwined with the music of Lawrence Welk.

I could see her point, but I still looked forward to an interview with the local paper. I would be modest, almost to a fault. I would not mention Jim Beam whiskey. The reporter would try to be objective, but he wouldn't be able to hide his admiration for my equity.

Loaded for Raccoon

WHEN THE RACCOONS started getting at the garbage cans next to the old house we go to in the summer, I naturally consulted the man in our town we call the Old Timer. He's the one who told me that we could assure ourselves of clear water by keeping a trout in the well, although, as it turned out, I couldn't find a trout except for a smoked trout that some guests from the city brought as a sort of house gift, and I didn't think it would be terribly gracious of me to toss that down the well, even assuming a smoked trout would do the trick. He's also the one who's always saying things like, "A porcupine that looks kinda cross-eyed will attack a house cat lickety-split."

"You already tried red onions, have you?" the Old Timer said when I told him about my raccoon problem. I really hate it when the Old Timer asks questions like that. The only acceptable answer is something like, "Well, naturally, that's the first thing I did, but for some reason it didn't work; must be the wet spring we had for onions

is all I can think of." If, instead, you say, "Well, no . . . ,"
the Old Timer is going to shake his head for a while without saying anything, as if he's determined not to allow
wholesale galloping ignorance to upset him.

"Well, no . . . ," I said when the Old Timer asked me
about red onions. He shook his head slowly for so long
that I thought he might be having some sort of attack.

Naturally I hadn't tried red onions. I didn't even know
what trying red onions meant. Did you festoon each
garbage can with red onions, as if you were decorating a
squat plastic Christmas tree? Did you plant a semicircle
of red onions around the garbage can area the way in-
fantrymen set up a defense perimeter of concertina
barbed wire? Did you sit at a darkened window until the
patter of little paws indicated that the time had come to
fling red onions at approaching raccoons?

What I had tried was tying down the garbage can lids
— until, on the morning of the weekly garbage pickup, I
found myself unable to get the knots undone and stood
there helplessly while the garbage collectors, with a cheerful wave, continued down the road. Then I secured the
lids by means of those stretchable cords with hooks on
the ends — I have some for lashing things to the roof
rack of the car — but it turned out that the raccoons
could pull the lids up far enough to get their paws in
there and pull out eighty or ninety square yards of crab
shells and melon rinds and milk cartons.

"A raccoon gets ten yards from half a red onion, he'll
turn tail and run, sure as shootin'," the Old Timer said.

I hate it when he says "sure as shootin'." I tried red
onions anyway, though — cut in half, as the Old Timer
had instructed, and placed on top of the lid with the cut

side up. The raccoons ate them, except for the skins,
which they mixed into some coffee grounds and spread on
the rosebush.

I wasn't surprised. The Old Timer is usually wrong. He
never admits it, of course. One time he told us that a
scarecrow with a red hat would keep deer out of the
garden, sure as shootin'. So we put a scarecrow out there,
and put a red hat on it, and the deer came the next night
and treated our garden like a salad bar. A neighbor who
happened to be awake in the early dawn hours (maybe
he was sitting at a darkened window waiting to fling red
onions at raccoons) noticed that one of the big bucks was
wearing a red hat when it left. I told the Old Timer that
the deer had demolished our entire lettuce crop, and he
said, "Yup, I suppose they did."

While I was testing my next plan, my wife and
daughters told me that I was forbidden to use violence on
the raccoons.

"This will only startle them," I said, secretly hoping
that it would do a lot more. My plan was to set mousetraps just under the garbage can lids. The raccoons pull
up the lids as much as my stretch-cords allow. They stick
their little paws in there and feel around, hoping to find
some chicken bones with peanut butter on them to spread
on the porch. Powee! I should have known that the gang
of raccoon apologists I live with would object. A few days
before, they had objected when I talked about putting the
fish heads I use as crab bait into a bait bag — a heavy
mesh bag that keeps the crabs already in the trap from
eating up the bait while still more crabs are being attracted. They said it would be cruel and deceitful.

I tried to tell them that there is no way you can be

deceitful to a crab. Crabs don't think. ("Hey, this smells like a good fish head. I'll just crawl into this place, even though it seems a little like the place that Uncle Manny crawled into just before he disappeared forever. Hey . . . Hey, wait a minute! I've been deceived!") No bait bags, they said, and no mousetraps.

So I gave it to them straight about raccoons. I told them that raccoons are about the meanest animals around. I happened to know from reading Albert Payson Terhune's books about collies that raccoons drown puppy dogs, just for sport.

"Don't be silly," my wife said. "Raccoons are so cute."

"That's what the puppy dogs think," I said. And puppy dogs do think, all the time. ("Hey, these cute little guys want to play in the water. This is fun! Hey . . . Hey, I've been de——glub, glub, glub.")

It was no use. They wouldn't give in. That's why I finally used a padlock on my garbage cans. I wanted to use a key lock, but the Old Timer said that a raccoon could pick a key lock nine times out of ten.

"He's probably wrong," I said to my wife.

"Maybe not," she said. "He didn't say 'sure as shootin'.' "

So I put on a combination lock, on the advice of the Old Timer. He said, "A raccoon's cunning, but he's got no head for figures."

Diseases of the Mighty

October 19, 1985

I READ IN AN Associated Press interview with John Z. DeLorean that he now talks "as if emerging from a long illness, a disease called egomania." Apparently, he had quite a bout of it. I gather from the A.P. piece that he's feeling better now — the newspaper I saw ran the piece under the headline DELOREAN IS RECOVERING SLOWLY FROM DIVORCE, LOSS OF COMPANY — but he still seems to require regular doses of evangelical Christianity and humble pie in order to avoid a recurrence. Swallowing his medicine right in front of the A.P. reporter, DeLorean said, "I believe I deserve what happened to me," leaving open for the moment the question of whether the investors and employees deserve what happened to them.

Naturally, I was relieved to hear that DeLorean is out of the woods; it's a pity, though, that the disease wasn't diagnosed and treated at an earlier stage. When someone is coming down with egomania, there must be symptoms that an alert diagnostician can spot: model-dating, maybe, or cosmetic surgery, or a tendency to name things after oneself.

I suppose a lot of people were surprised to read that egomania was a disease. Not me. I realize, of course, that it's not the sort of disease you can get reimbursed for on the office medical plan, or the kind of disease you can mention to the boss as the reason you didn't come in for a couple of days ("So I, in my superb wisdom, decided to get into a toga, and by the time I found a pedestal worthy of having me stand on it . . ."). Still, it has become clear to me that these days there are a lot of diseases that the diagnosticians of simpler times might have missed while under the impression that what they were witnessing was just rotten behavior.

The talk shows are stuffed full of sufferers who have regained their health — congressmen who suffered through a serious spell of boozing and skirt-chasing, White House aides who were stricken cruelly with overweening ambition, movie stars and baseball players who came down with acute cases of wanting to trash hotel rooms while under the influence of recreational drugs. Most of them have found God, or at least a publisher.

When I hear that one of the recovered is going to be interviewed on television, I always tune in. I have a taste for the sordid stuff. As I read in the newspapers about all of the business executives these days whose corporations have, in the normal course of business, kited checks and bribed foreign governments and bilked the Defense Department and diddled the books, I am cheered by the thought that in a year or so, if the usual publication schedules work out, we'll be able to see them on television, thanking the Lord for their cures and acknowledging the concerned inquiries of the host about the current state of their health ("Well, Steve, it's like emerging from a disease called untrammeled greed").

In simpler times, a business executive who was caught following a number of corporate policies that happened to be felonious would have had a completely different response: he did it for the stockholders. He had a sacred obligation to make certain that the stockholders had the greatest possible return on their investment, and avoiding huge disposal costs by simply dumping the chemical wastes out behind the shed was one way of fulfilling that obligation. In those days, every corporation executive had a good angel on one shoulder ("I know how old Ted McNeil, who built this company, would have approached this question, because Ted knew every man on the line by his first name and believed that quality was the only . . .") and on the other shoulder 80,000 stockholders yelling, "Cheat, bribe, pollute, steal, kick, bite, scratch!"

According to the accepted model of that era, the president of, say, Stinko Chemicals would have, if left to his own inclinations, priced industrial-strength sewer cleaner at just slightly above what it cost the company to manufacture it, which might put the price at about 18¢ a barrel. But then he thinks of a stockholder, a widow in a small town in Georgia who has her husband's insurance money in Stinko shares. He imagines her going out to the mailbox to pick up her dividend check, opening the envelope with great anticipation, and then looking pathetically dejected as she realizes that the dividend has gone down and that she will have to abandon her one remaining pleasure — playing the slots at the Legion hall on Friday nights. So he prices the barrel of sewer cleaner at $34.95.

As it happens, $34.95 a barrel is the price that four of his competitors are charging. The president of Stinko knows that old Ted McNeil would have undercut the competition ("We'll build it better, and we'll sell it cheaper,

and we won't compromise on . . ."), but he is also aware
that he has that widow from Georgia and 79,999 other
widows tap-dancing on his other shoulder. So he gets together with his four competitors and fixes the price. If
he gets caught, he can tell the truth: he did it for the
stockholders.

That's not the way it works now. When the new male-
factors have their go at the airwaves, they'll have to talk
about the illnesses they managed to conquer. "I found that
I was a compulsive briber," one of them might say to the
interviewer. "And if the Lord hadn't cured me I'd probably
be laying ten bucks on you right now to get a better camera
angle." The others, recovered from afflictions like egomania and chronic hyperambition, will nod in sympathy,
like people at a prayer meeting who can empathize with
the reformed drunk even though gambling happens to
be their own cross. The interviewer will give them his
forgiveness and bless their books.

I'll be watching, and not just for the sordid stuff. I have
long entertained the fantasy that some interviewer someday is going to turn to one of the recovered sufferers and
say, "But isn't this just another way of saying that you're
a wretched little worm who acted despicably just to rise in
your dreadful firm or impress the girls?" Of course, the
recoveree will simply say, "Yes, you're right. I was suffering from wormlike behavior. I deserve everything that
happened to me."

To Catch a Wonk

November 9, 1985

I HOPE STUDENTS of the language noticed a quote in the *New York Times* recently that might have marked the first time anybody has ever used the word "yuppies" in a way that assumes them to be desirable rather than silly. The person quoted was one of the purchasers of Grossinger's, the Borscht Belt resort renowned for its contribution to American stand-up comedy and Jewish gastric distress. He said that the new ownership would be creating "more of a yuppie-type of facility." At first I thought it might have been a typo. Why would the owner of a resort tell potential guests that what they might run into at his place is a bunch of yuppies? Even if he secretly hoped to appeal to people who could be categorized as yuppies — according to the *Times*, the new management's financial papers refer to its target audience as "upscale families of the baby boom generation" — why would he come right out and call them that? As far as I know, the old owners of Grossinger's never said anything like, "We're trying to run a resort where people who are probably a little overweight already can make disgusting pigs out of themselves three meals a day."

"Maybe some people don't consider 'yuppie' a derogatory term," my wife said.

She's always saying things like that. I might as well reveal right here and now that it's her influence I blame for the children's excessive tolerance. "Yuppie" is obviously a derogatory term. If it weren't, why would so many people use the phrase "crawling with yuppies"? I have used that phrase any number of times myself, and I can assure you that I meant it in a derogatory way every single time. I have used it most often in restaurants that are so packed with "upscale families of the baby boom generation" that respectable citizens are forced to wait for tables. What is particularly maddening about such places is the knowledge that a lot of the yuppies are there because they actually enjoy waiting; they like to stand at the bar and talk about what they're doing with their IRA money. Finding yourself in a crowd that was attracted by the prospect of crowdedness is a little like finding yourself in a dreadful traffic jam just after you've discovered that you're on the wrong road. It's perfectly understandable that someone in that position might respond by muttering, "This goddamned place is crawling with yuppies."

My wife reminded me that some people these days use the word "nerd" in a way that's not derogatory, particularly in the term "computer nerd." Not me. As it happens, I almost never call anyone a nerd — I'm partial to the term "wonk" — but when I do, you can be certain that I mean it as an insult. I'm not at all impressed by those movies about computer nerds in high school who triumph in some improbable way over the jocks, because I know the secret reason those movies are made: nearly everybody who makes movies in Hollywood was himself a nerd in high school. Not a computer nerd, just a nerd. These Hollywood people turn out computer-nerd movies to make us think it's O.K. to be a nerd. (It isn't.) These days, of course, they do their best to act cool — wearing their shirts unbuttoned to their *pupik*, handing out cocaine as dinner-party favors — but they know who they are. I believe it was Carl Jung who said, "Everybody's who he was in high school," to which Wilhelm Reich, that shrewd old cockamamie gentleman, countered, "A wonk is a wonk — let's face it."

It's interesting that Reich used the term "wonk" (or, in the original German, *Vonk*), because the term I was familiar with in college was not "wonk" but "weenie." They are synonymous, and they are both derogatory. I can't imagine anyone telling the *New York Times* that he and his partners were interested in creating "more of a weenie-type of facility." Even my wife and children, in their most intense periods of mad-dog tolerance, could not have said something like, "I met an interesting wonk today."

In the late 1960s, when some colleges were themselves in an intense period of mad-dog tolerance, I returned to the campus and found that the word "weenie" had disappeared. When I reported that to a classmate of mine, he said, "What's their word for a weenie?"

"That's just it," I said. "They don't seem to have a word for 'weenie.'"

"In that case," he said, "they're *all* weenies."

The spirit of the late 1960s is now gone, of course. Everyone has a word for weenie again. The latest one I've heard is "dweeb," as in "He's a total dweeb." Apparently, a total dweeb is the only kind of dweeb you can be. There's no dweeb spectrum. Nobody can be just a tad dweebish any more than he could have been a little bit wonklike. As Freud himself might have said, "Once a dweeb, always a dweeb — and that goes double for Reich."

I'm not sure how many yuppies used to be dweebs or nerds. (They are not old enough to have been weenies or wonks.) The last statistic I heard was 38 percent — although, as I understand it, that figure was arrived at by factoring in a wimp quotient, which I find completely irrelevant. It's easy enough to spot nerds among people who make movies in Hollywood — they're the ones with the unbuttoned shirts who are handing out cocaine — but it's more difficult with yuppies. When people are discussing IRAs, they tend to seem pretty much alike. Also, any survey-taker is aware that it could be dangerous to offend yuppies by asking too many personal questions, since all of them have a racquetball racquet on their persons at all times.

The other interesting question is whether yuppies are preferable to dweebs. I wonder. There's no doubt in my mind that high school nerds are preferable to people who make movies in Hollywood. Which means, I suppose, that I can see the possibility of using "nerd" or even "yuppie" in a sense that's not derogatory, at least in a comparative way. I wouldn't want that known among the people I went to college with, of course. It might make them think I've become a weenie.

The Chicken à la King
Question

November 30, 1985

I'VE BEEN WONDERING for a long time where all the chicken à la king went. A few years ago, I began to think that the government might have it stored somewhere — in huge silos, maybe, or in those salt caves in Kansas where they keep surplus rutabagas and old Army morning reports. When I come across a cluster of those silos on the plains, I figure maybe two of them have chicken à la king and the third one has beef stroganoff and the fourth one is filled to the top with Nehru jackets. I've been wondering for a long time where all the Nehru jackets went.

There must be billions of gallons of chicken à la king somewhere. There was a time — in the 1950s, say — when the whole country seemed to be awash in chicken à la king. Thousands of Kiwanians ate it at Kiwanis luncheons. Kiwanians ate so much chicken à la king that whenever I heard them sing their song, "I'd Rather Be a Kiwanian Than in Any Other Club," I expected to hear a few lines in there about the health-giving qualities of the dish that was giving strength and succor to all Kiwanians everywhere.

> There's nothing can defeat us,
> Whatever life may bring.
> 'Cause we can go and eat us
> Some chicken à la king.
> So I'd rather be a Kiwanian than in any other club.

In those days, rich people of the sort who were listed in the social register ate a lot of chicken à la king, doled out of silver serving bowls at wedding receptions and coming-out parties by waiters who looked snottier than the guests. This was not chicken à la king left over from the Kiwanis luncheon; a lot of the towns where rich society people live are so fancy that they don't even have a Kiwanis. This was brand-new chicken à la king. I had the opportunity to witness rich people eating it because one of them was my college roommate — Thatcher Baxter Hatcher, known as Tush. I ate chicken à la king at Tush Hatcher's wedding. I ate chicken à la king at the coming-out party for Tush Hatcher's sister Baxter Thatcher Hatcher. (She was known as Caca, since a suitor who was whispering sweet nothings into the ear of someone called Baxter might suddenly get the feeling he was talking to the chief executive officer.) There was so much chicken à la king at Caca Hatcher's party that, as I danced the fox trot to the bouncy debutante music of Lester Lanin and his No Sex on the Dance Floor Orchestra, I half expected a chanteuse to step to the microphone and sing:

> Our sacred club is safe
> From those of non-WASP blood.
> 'Cause none of them apply:
> They wouldn't eat this crud.

There was a time, in fact, when I thought that it might be chicken à la king consumption that was causing rich society people to talk without opening their mouths. I knew that the sauce that chicken à la king floats around in could get kind of gluelike, particularly when it sat around in silver serving bowls for a while, and I thought it might be bonding the rich people's teeth together. (I mean, of course, a single rich person's upper plate to his lower plate, not one rich person's teeth to another rich person's teeth. Although, now that I come to think of it, Tush Hatcher's mother talked a bit like her teeth were bonded to the teeth of Tush's father, or somebody.) I dropped the theory when I realized that my cousin Oscar, who was a mad-dog Kiwanian, consumed as much chicken à la king as any rich person, and he didn't talk without opening his mouth. In fact, Oscar erred a bit in the other direction, particularly when he was talking and eating chicken à la king at the same time.

In those days I would sometimes say to my college roommate, "Tush, you rich people eat chicken à la king like it was going out of style." And that's what happened. It went out of style. They must have been stoking up, knowing that. Those rich people weren't so dumb. They just sounded dumb, because of having their teeth bonded together from eating chicken à la king.

So what happened to it? It must be out in those silos. The way I see this, the government probably tried to fob it off on some poor people in some place like India, and they wouldn't eat it. They didn't want to seem ungrateful, so they told the State Department people that the chicken is sacred in India. The real reason was that the Indians thought chicken à la king tasted like the sort of thing

WASPs eat in their clubs; during the Raj, the British ate a dish very much like chicken à la king in their clubs in order to keep the Indians from applying, although they called it Aunt Nigel's Boots. To this day, though, a lot of State Department people think that the chicken is sacred in India. What India really wanted from the silos were the Nehru jackets, but State wouldn't release them unless the Indians also agreed to accept a thousand carloads of bell-bottom blue jeans.

When the current fashion for American cooking began, some people thought it was a conspiracy by the government to get rid of all that chicken à la king. It wasn't. Here is how this fashion for American cooking started: Bloomingdale's ran out of countries. That's right. It had already held a Fall Festival of France and a Celebration of Japan and a Wonders of India month. There weren't many countries left. You can't have a Chad Celebration or a Guyana Festival. So Bloomingdale's celebrated America, and the rest is, as they say, goat cheese.

Also, the restaurants that have sprung up during the fashion for American cooking don't serve chicken à la king. They serve fried chicken. They serve chicken pot pie. No chicken à la king. Is it still out there in the silos? I'm not sure. Not long ago, on a particularly fancy airline menu, I came across an item called Poulet aux Champignons Supreme. I asked the stewardess what she thought it was. She looked around furtively. She drew closer. Then she said, in almost a whisper, "Chicken à la king."

Hate Thy Neighbor

April 6, 1986

MY WIFE KEEPS TELLING ME that I don't really hate the neighbor of ours who talks a lot about the importance of trim and gutter maintenance. I've had this problem with my wife before.

She is the person who insisted that I was only joking when I said several years ago that people who sell macramé ought to be dyed a natural color and hung out to dry. She is the person who tried to shush me when I told a man who pushed ahead of me in an airport line that only certified wonks wear designer blue jeans.

It is my wife who argued that I had no legal standing for making a citizen's arrest of someone for performing mime in public. Can you blame me for blaming her for the children's excessive tolerance?

I haven't done any trim and gutter maintenance in so long that I'm no longer quite certain what there is about them that needs to be maintained. I also feel that way about the points and plugs on the car. I know they're important, but I can't quite remember why. The same neighbor — he can be called Elwood here, although around the house I always refer to him as Old Glittering Gutters — cannot see my car without patting it on the hood as if it were an exceedingly large Airedale and saying, "When was the last time you had a good look at the points and plugs?"

"I'd rather not say," I always reply.

It's none of his business. His points and plugs are, I'm sure, sharply pointed and firmly plugged in, or whatever they're supposed to be. His trim and gutters are, it goes without saying, carefully maintained. You could probably eat out of Elwood's gutters if that's the kind of person you were. I hate him.

"You don't really hate him," my wife said. "You may think he's a little too well organized for your tastes, and you may not want him over for dinner all the time. But you don't hate him."

Wrong. Elwood has a list of what's in his basement. He says the list is invaluable. He wonders why I don't have a list of what's in my basement. He doesn't seem to understand that if I made such a list, it would have to be a list of what *might* be in my basement, and it would have to include the possibility of crocodiles. Elwood's list is cross-indexed. A man who has a cross-indexed list of what's in his basement is not a little too well organized, he's hateful.

The other day Elwood asked me what sort of system I use to label my circuit breakers. I tried to remain calm. I made every effort to analyze his question in a manner detached enough to prevent physical violence. I tried to think of reasons why Elwood would assume that someone who had already confessed ignorance as to the whereabouts of his 1984 gasoline credit card receipts ("There might be some stuffed in the glove compartment there with the spare points and plugs, Elwood, but I hate to open that thing unless it's a real emergency") would have his circuit breakers labeled at all, let alone have them labeled according to some system.

I calculated, as precisely as I could, what chance there was that a jury, learning of the question that preceded the crime, would bring in a verdict of not guilty on the grounds that the strangling of Elwood had clearly been a crime of passion.

"The system I'm using now," I finally said, "is to label them Sleepy, Grumpy, Sneezy, Happy, Dopey, Doc, and Bashful. However, I've given a lot of thought to switching to a system under which I would label them Dasher, Dancer, Prancer, Vixen, Comet, Cupid, Donder, and Bruce. I'm holding up my final decision until a friend of mine who has access to a large computer runs some probability studies."

"Probability of what?" Elwood said. I noticed that as he asked the question he retreated a step or two toward his own house.

"Just probability," I said.

When I got back inside my house, I told my wife about the conversation and about the possibility that Elwood now believed me to be not simply slovenly in the extreme but completely bonkers.

"Poor man," she said. "He probably thinks you're dangerous."

"He may be right," I said.

"You have to try to think of Elwood as a human being," my wife said. "Someone with feelings, and a wife and children who love him."

"I suspect his children sell macramé in public," I said. "Or maybe they're in a troupe of those street-corner mimes who've somehow got it in their heads that passers-by are longing to see people with white paint on their faces pretend to walk slowly against the wind."

"Also," she said, "it really wouldn't be such a bad idea to label the circuit breakers."

I looked at her for a while. "You're right, of course," I finally said. I got a felt-tipped pen, went to the circuit breaker box, and started right in: "Sleepy, Grumpy, Sneezy . . ."

Invasion of the
Limo-Stretchers

April 13, 1986

I PINNED WHAT Pam Blessinger said about rich people
on my bulletin board. For a few months now, it has been
in the section I reserve for permanent display, right next
to a *Wizard of Oz* quotation that somehow comforts dis-
placed Midwesterners in New York City by stating what
should be increasingly obvious: "Toto, I don't think we're
in Kansas anymore."

Pam Blessinger spoke as president of the residents'
association of New York's Roosevelt Island, which is in the
East River in a spot usually described as under the shadow
of the Fifty-ninth Street Bridge. Developed ten years ago
as a middle-income "new town," Roosevelt Island has
become a quiet, family sort of place that one of Blessinger's fellow residents described to the *New York Times*
as "an island of Indiana in the middle of Manhattan."

Blessinger was quoted in the *Times* in opposition to a
proposed expansion of the development which would in-

clude what looked to her suspiciously like luxury apartments. "We're not against white or black or purple," she said. "What we're against is rich people."

There. She said it. The rest of us have been pussyfooting around this for years, afraid of being called prejudiced. Not Mrs. B. She could envision the peaceful lanes of her little island jammed with triple-parked stretch limousines waiting in front of restaurants where a plate of spaghetti costs $18 and change. She could see the day when respectable citizens who have to get up and go to work the next morning would be awakened in the middle of the night by the braying of rich people being dropped off after charity balls: "It was marvelous, darling!" "Wasn't it marvelous, darling?" "Yes, it was marvelous, darling!"

Mrs. B. said out loud what the rest of us have been thinking: Those people can ruin a neighborhood lickety-split.

No, we are not prejudiced. We wouldn't mind one or two rich people, but these days the supply of them seems inexhaustible. The *Forbes* list of the country's four hundred richest people is so jammed with the truly loaded that someone with, say, only $145 million to his name can't even get mentioned. He has to walk around uncertified by *Forbes*, like some sort of deadbeat.

As seems to be true of so many recent developments in American life, this surfeit of richies has come as a surprise to me. When I was growing up, one of the most important things about truly rich people was that there weren't very many of them. Also, my high school teachers told us that people like the Rockefellers had grabbed their piles before the tax laws made it impossible to amass huge personal fortunes.

So why have so many people become as rich as the Rockefellers? Is it possible that these rich people know something about the tax laws that my high school teachers didn't know?

Most of the rich people are in New York. I don't care what *Forbes* says about where they live. They're here. We've got Texas rich people and California rich people and Colorado rich people. We've got rich people with new money and rich people with old money and rich people whose money just needs to sit in the window for a few days and ripen in the sun. There's no variety of rich people we don't have in overstock. New York has more rich people than some cities have people.

For a while, I thought other places might be sending us their rich people. ("Listen, if Frank down at the Savings and Loan doesn't quit talking about how many Jaguars he owns, we're just going to have to put him in the next shipment to New York.") It even occurred to me that whoever is in charge of these other places might have misread the poem on the Statue of Liberty, which definitely says, "Give me you tired, your *poor*." People make mistakes.

Then I realized that the rich people were coming here on their own hook. They are swarming into New York because they want to be with people who are like they are — rich. There are a lot of places around the country, after all, where someone who is driven around in a stretched-out Cadillac limousine might be made light of ("Will you look at that thing old Albert's got himself? Don't you figure he must think he's always on his way to a funeral?"). For all I know, there are places around the country where someone who is driven around in a stretched-out Cadillac limousine might have rocks thrown at him.

"Send 'em back where they came from," a taxi driver who was hauling me up the East Side Drive one day said as he struggled to get around a gaggle of limos. He had devised a rich-people repatriation plan that sounded very much like Fidel Castro's Mariel boatlift, except that he'd use private jets instead of fishing boats.

"But that would be prejudiced and unfair," I said, although not terribly forcefully.

"Then send them to Idaho or Iowa or one of those places where there aren't any stoplights," he said. It is taken for granted by most New York taxi drivers that all states beginning with *I* are interchangeable parts of the same vast unpeopled prairie.

"Send 'em to Illinois," he said as we passed under the Fifty-ninth Street Bridge. "Or Indiana." At that moment he looked out onto the East River. "Or maybe just Roosevelt Island."

Did the Marcoses
Seem Rich?

April 27, 1986

IF YOU HAVE ALL finally finished talking about Mrs. Marcos's shoes, I'd like to discuss this situation on a higher level. No, I'm not referring to Mrs. Marcos's belts and accessories. The higher level I'm talking about is White House level.

While the rest of you have been scrutinizing Mrs. M.'s footwear supply, wondering out loud how 2,700 pair of shoes could be broken in without the use of political prisoners, I have been analyzing what Ronald Reagan said when reporters asked him if he had ever happened to notice, back before the fall of the House of Imelda, that Ferdinand Marcos seemed to have an awful lot of disposable income for a man on a government salary. For years, after all, the Reagans and the Marcoses were, if I may use the phrase with all due respect, thick as thieves.

It's true, of course, that the President is accustomed to being in the company of people who live pretty high off the hog. In the movie business, as I understand it, even people who are having what they might describe as a little cash-flow problem think nothing of diverting the insurance premium money toward a down payment on a new Jaguar. So it's not as if the President would take special notice if someone he palled around with happened to have a nice set of wheels and maybe a Rolex to encourage promptness and good work habits.

You'd think, though, that President Reagan might have been a little suspicious about how the Marcos family managed to acquire Manhattan office buildings and snatch clean the shelves of Paris dress designers on a salary that Reagan himself has described as "extremely modest." Just consider the sort of speculation you've heard about those people in your neighborhood who somehow, on one modest salary, keep three kids in private school, make constant trips to Europe, redecorate the activity room almost annually, and maintain a country house that has a swimming pool and five acres of pasture and an Arabian mare named Kimberly:

"But how much could a junior high school guidance counselor make?"

"Maybe she comes from money."

"Nobody who lives in Day-Glo stretch pants comes from money."

When Orval Faubus, the one-time governor of Arkansas, was asked how he managed to build a $200,000 house after a career in public service that never paid him more than $10,000 a year, he explained in one word: thrift. But it turns out that not even President Reagan, who's noted for giving his friends the benefit of the doubt, believed that Marcos could stretch a buck quite that far.

According to what the President told reporters, he had been under the impression that Marcos was well-off when he took office and had acquired some wealth legitimately "by way of investments." That's the answer I've been analyzing while the rest of you were speculating in a disrespectful way about how many pair of shoes Nancy Reagan owns, and the conclusion I came to is that people like the Marcoses and the Reagans must come across a different sort of investment opportunity than people like you and me.

When Reagan talks about investments, he obviously is not talking about one of those banks that offer you 7½ percent on your IRA money plus a toaster if you agree not to withdraw a penny for threescore years plus ten. He is not talking about the sort of deal your brother-in-law offered when he heard about a hot computers issue from a guy down at the garage and said he could get you in on the ground floor if you could show your appreciation by advancing him what he intended to invest himself, just till he could put his hands on some cash.

What I imagine President Reagan imagining, as the Marcos family acquired enough money to buy up country estates and pop $10 or $20 million at a crack into Swiss bank accounts, was a different sort of investment opportunity: "We'd be happy to guarantee a minimum return of 800 percent on your money by the end of the month, Mr. Marcos, and of course this thing could really take off."

What amazes me is the restraint our President displayed as the CIA reports of Marcos wealth piled up on his desk. In President Reagan's shoes (thirty-five pair), I wouldn't have been able to control my curiosity. If I, as the President of the United States, met with the President of the Philippines in a summit conference, I would have pushed aside all of the reports having to do with the Philippine economy and the American military bases and the communist insurgency. "Let's get down to it, Ferdinand," I would have said. "Who the hell is your broker?"

Spelling Yiffniff

MY FATHER USED TO offer an array of prizes for anyone who could spell yiffniff. That's not how to spell it, of course — yiffniff. I'm just trying to let you know what it sounds like, in case you'd like to take a crack at it yourself. Don't get your hopes up: this is a spelling word that once defied some of the finest twelve-year-old minds Kansas City had to offer.

The prizes were up for grabs any time my father drove us to a Boy Scout meeting. After a while, all he had to say to start the yiffniff attempts was "Well?"

"Y-i . . ." some particularly brave kid like Dogbite Davis would say.

"Wrong," my father would say, in a way that somehow made it sound like "Wrong, dummy."

"How could I be wrong already?" Dogbite would say.

"Wrong," my father would repeat. "Next."

Sometimes he would begin the ride by calling out the prizes he was offering: ". . . a new Schwinn three-speed, a trip to California, a lifetime pass to Kansas City Blues baseball games, free piano lessons for a year, a new pair of shoes." No matter what the other prizes were, the list always ended with "a new pair of shoes."

Some of the prizes were not tempting to us. We weren't interested in shoes. We would have done anything to avoid free piano lessons for a year. Still, we were desperate to spell yiffniff.

"L-l . . ." Eddie Williams began one day.

"Wrong," my father said. "Next."

"That's Spanish," Eddie said, "the double *L* that sounds like a *y*."

"This is English," my father said. "Next."

Sometimes someone would ask what yiffniff meant.

"You don't have to give the definition to get the prizes," my father would say. "Just spell it."

As far as I could gather, yiffniff didn't have a definition. It was a word that existed solely to be spelled. My father had invented it for that purpose.

Occasionally some kid in the car would make an issue out of yiffniff's origins. "But you made it up!" he'd tell my father, in an accusing tone.

"Of course I made it up," my father would reply. "That's why I know how to spell it."

"But it could be spelled a million ways."

"All of them are wrong except my way," my father would say. "It's my word."

If you're thinking that my father, who had never shared the secret of how to spell his word, could have simply called any spelling we came up with wrong and thus avoided handing out the prizes, you never knew my father. His views on honesty made the Boy Scout position on that subject seem wishy-washy. There was no doubt among us that my father knew how to spell yiffniff and would award the prizes to anyone who spelled it that way. But nobody seemed able to do it.

Finally, we brought in a ringer — my cousin Keith, from Salina, who had reached the finals of the Kansas State Spelling Bee. (Although Keith's memory has always differed from mine on this point, I'm sure I was saying even then that the word he missed in the finals was "hayseed.") We told my father that Keith, who was visiting Kansas City, wanted to go to a Scout meeting with us to brush up on some of his knots.

"Well?" my father said, when the car was loaded.

"Yiffniff," my cousin Keith said clearly, announcing the assigned word in the spelling bee style. "Y-y . . ."

Y-y! Using *y* both as a consonant and as a vowel! What a move! We looked at my father for a response. He said nothing. Emboldened, Keith picked up the pace: "Y-y-g-h-k-n-i-p-h."

For a few moments the car was silent. Then my father said, "Wrong. Next."

Suddenly the car was bedlam as we began arguing about where our plans had gone wrong. "Maybe we should have got the guy who knew how to spell 'hayseed,'" Dogbite said. We argued all the way to the Scout meeting, but it was the sort of argument that erupts on a team that has already lost the game. We knew Keith had been our best shot.

Keith now teaches English to college students. He presumably has scholarly credentials that go beyond spelling, but he still worries about yiffniff. Not long ago, while we were talking about something else, he suddenly said, "Maybe I should have put a hyphen between yiff and niff."

"No, it doesn't have a hyphen," I said.

"How do you know?"

"Because the other day one of my kids spelled it your way except with a hyphen, and I had to tell her she was wrong," I said. "It's a shame. She's really had her eye on winning that new pair of shoes."

Flimsy Envelopes

May 11, 1986

ALL RIGHT, PARENTS, those of you who have ever secretly opened mail addressed to any of your children please raise your hands.

Yes, I'm talking about mail such as letters from college admission offices. Yes, I'm talking about mail such as the letter to your daughter that looked as if it might have come from the boy you banned from the house after you found out that he was the recording secretary of the local outlaw motorcycle gang — that envelope that seemed to have axle grease smudges in the corner and showed indications of having been addressed by someone who thinks the word "street" begins with a *c*.

Is your hand up there, sir — you in the back row? Sir? I was asking if your hand is up or if, for reasons we needn't go into right now if you'd rather not, you happen to be trying to scratch the inside of your left earlobe with your right hand.

I'm still having a little trouble getting an accurate count here. The red-haired woman in the corner may be putting her hand up part-way or she may be doing her imitation of a Canada goose who has lost the use of one wing. Let's be open with each other, folks.

What was that, sir? Yes, the gentleman in the front row. No need to mumble. We can be open with each other here, sir. If you suspect that you might have behaved like a rather brutish and high-handed parent, and you seek the company of other rather brutish and high-handed parents, I'd like to assure you that you've come to the right place.

Whisper in my ear? Well, sir, if you insist. What was that? "Does it count if the envelope falls open in your hand?"

Could we please have some comment on that from the group? I'd like to hear what you think about this. As I understand what this gentleman is saying, he happened to go through the mail before his son arrived home from high school, he picked up a letter addressed to his son by a firm called Hideously Noisy Rock Music Equipment, Inc., the envelope fell open in his hand, and the letter unfolded itself to reveal that his son had used the computer-programming school money for a down payment on a $30,000 synthesizer and had signed a waiver releasing the sellers of any responsibility if the synthesizer in its salsa mode caused any structural damage to the house.

All right, does everyone here find that plausible — that business about the envelope falling open in his hand? Oh, everyone does. Well, O.K. Fine. Oh, yes, one question from the woman in the corner. In case you couldn't hear that, sir: she would like to know if you spoke to your son about the synthesizer, or perhaps even chastised him.

Oh, I see. Yes. Well, then. Perhaps someone near the back of the room there could dial 911 and say that there's

a man here who would like to turn himself in for a major felony.

If we can just move ahead, I'd like to bring up the big-envelope/small-envelope question as it relates to college admission letters. As many of you know, there's a theory that a large, fat envelope is an acceptance, because it obviously contains various forms and announcements needed by a prospective freshman, that a small envelope is likely to be a rejection — and that there is, therefore, no reason for a parent to open the envelope. Does everyone agree with that? Oh.

What was that, madam? Well, that's an interesting theory. What you're saying, as I understand it, is that some colleges, just as a little joke, might send someone a large, fat envelope that turns out to hold a one-page rejection letter and a lot of old newspapers stuffed in there to make you think you've been sent dormitory forms and the cal endar for the fall semester.

Well, how many people find that plausible? How m of you believe that a major American educational i tution is likely to stuff its rejection-letter envelopes old newspapers just to torment the parents of st who apply? Oh, I see: all of you, even the gentlem had the envelope from the synthesizer company f as he held it. You needn't hold up two hands, see. The handcuffs.

So, if we can just move on to methods. I everyone here carefully steams open the e then reseals it with glue. No? You what? We sir. That strikes me as, well, rather bru handed. I can't believe anyone else would thing, but let's get a count. How many

open the envelope and then claim that the dog got at it?

The gentleman in the second row: sir, are you raising your hand in a rather tentative way or do you have a nasty sprain that requires you to keep your elbow above the hairline at all times? I'm having a little trouble getting an accurate count. Up or down. Let's be open with each other, folks.

Castro Forgotten, Alas

May 18, 1986

HOW DO YOU THINK Fidel Castro feels now that he never gets blamed for anything anymore? How do you think he feels seeing Muammar Khadafy get blamed for everything? I'll tell you how I think he feels: I think he hates it. I think we finally hit him where it hurts.

It used to be that whenever peasants in some Central American country started shooting back at the generals, the State Department said that Fidel Castro was exporting revolution. Drug problems in South Florida? Castro was to blame. Unrest in Africa? Castro did it.

Everything was blamed on Castro. Mudslides in California. The fact that you can't buy a decent tomato anymore. Was there an exceptionally high pollen count in Massapequa, Long Island, one day? It was Castro, exporting sneezes.

All of this gave Castro the sort of exalted status I still associate with a mischievous schoolmate of mine named Darrell Hamm, master of the MIRV spitball. Darrell's reputation for wicked pranks was so firmly established that he was routinely blamed for any atrocity visited upon the unfortunate Miss Hoffmeister in Latin class even on those occasions when he could have proven, if he had chosen to, that he spent the entire school day at Waldo Tap & Billiards.

Think of what it must have been like in the old days when Castro walked into a room filled with other heads of state — say, at a conference of the Organization of Neutralist Yankee-Bashers.

"Hey, Fidel, the Yankees were really mad at you when the steel industry in the industrial Midwest collapsed," the other Yankee-bashers would call out. "Hey, Fidel, you sure make them squeal when you did that drought in West Texas." Castro would smile knowingly, and wave in acknowledgment, and secretly wonder how you'd do a drought.

In those days, whenever his own people seemed in a rebellious mood over something like the shortage of consumer goods — Cubans, who have always been known as snappy dressers, hated standing in line to buy those clunky Czechoslovakian shoes — Castro could distract them by saying that the Yankees had finally got so mad at him that they were going to invade. Then everyone would get into uniform and go dig trenches for a while. After a couple of weeks most Cubans would begin to think that Czech shoes were at least snappier than combat boots, and that would be the end of the rebellion.

Can you imagine the response these days if Castro told the country that the Americans were so mad at him they might invade? "Get serious, Fidel," someone would say. "They might not even remember your name. And listen, while we're on the subject, do you think that just once you might be able to import shoes from a country where they're not under the impression that the shape of the human foot is a perfect square?"

When he's with other heads of state now, Castro must be in the position Darrell Hamm would have been in if the school authorities had suddenly quit blaming him for everything: we would have figured that he was angling to get Miss Hoffmeister to write him a recommendation letter for the fender-repair program at Vo-Tech.

I can just imagine Castro these days at a conference of the Organization of Neutralist Yankee-Bashers. One of the old-time Yankee-bashers puts his arm around Castro and says, "Listen, Fidel, we all understand. You have to watch your step. Those Yankees could crush you like a gnat."

"But I'm exporting just as much revolution as ever!" Fidel insists. "I even sent more sneezes to Massapequa!"

"The Yankees were really ticked off at Muammar for that last drop in the stock market," the old-timer says, as if Castro had not spoken.

"I deserved the blame for that," Castro says. "And also the flash flood in West Virginia."

The old-timer smiles, and says, "Nobody can do a flash flood, Fidel." Then he nearly snaps to attention. Muammar Khadafy has just walked into the room.

"Hey, Muammar, they were furious at you about the fall of the dollar against the yen," one head of state calls out as Fidel Castro chomps viciously on his cigar. "Boy, you really got their goat with that flash flood in West Virginia," someone else calls out.

"I thought you said nobody could do a flash flood," Fidel says to the old-timer, but the old-timer doesn't seem to hear.

"The Yankees blame Muammar for everything," the old-timer says, his voice filled with admiration. "He could get attacked anytime."

And, the way I imagine it, he does get attacked just a few days later. Fighter planes dive so close to Khadafy's tent that he can read their markings. The planes have Cuban markings. Fidel Castro sent them.

"I hate to wake him up just for that," Regan says.

"He is awake," Ed Meese says. "I just saw him wink and grin and give the thumbs-up sign."

"Well, let's tell him about the deficit," James Baker says.

"You know he doesn't want to hear about the deficit," Regan says. "The last time I tried to bring it up he told me that story again about the welfare mother who picks up her check in a Cadillac. I think if he tells me that story one more time I'm going to defect."

"We've got to tell him something," Larry Speakes says. "I can't keep telling these reporters that the President is being briefed if we never tell him anything."

"Gentlemen," Buchanan says. "I think I've got it." He rummages around in the bottom of his briefcase, picks up a slim file, and walks to the President's desk. "Mr. President," he says, rather formally, "Norwegians have committed whaling infractions."

The President winks and grins and gives the thumbs-up sign.

Important Volumes

MY FRIEND HOWARD CORKUM took David Stockman's book to the cottage the Corkums have at the beach, and immediately started talking about how guilty he felt about not reading it.

"I feel terrible about this," Howard said when I went to visit them a few days after they opened up the cottage for the summer. "Here I've spent $22.95 for a book I haven't even opened. I can't imagine why I bought it in the first place. I mean, it's not as if I've been a big fan of David Stockman. He looks like he was George Will's roommate in college and they had the only absolutely tidy room in the dormitory."

"Take it easy, Howard," I said. "You just got here. How do you know you won't read it before the end of the summer?"

"That's how I know," Howard said, pointing to a small mountain of thick volumes on the other side of the parlor. I couldn't see all the titles from where I was sitting, but I did make out *Keeping Faith: Memoirs of a President* by

Jimmy Carter and *The White House Years* by Henry S. Kissinger. "I haven't opened any of them," Howard said. "I feel just awful about this whole thing."

None of this surprised me. Every winter, Howard, feverish with good intentions, buys some pound-and-a-half political memoir that he describes as "important," and puts it aside to read when he gets to the beach cottage in the summer. He never seems to remember that what he actually does at the beach all summer is putter around in an old shed turning found objects like driftwood and lobster buoys into small pieces of furniture that, in the words of the mutual friend we call Marty Mean Tongue, "make you understand that certain found objects were meant to remain lost."

Sitting there in the Corkums' parlor, wobbling slightly on a chair Howard has fashioned from railroad ties, I regretted not having thought to phone Howard's wife, Edna, last winter and suggest that she clip any mention of the Stockman book from Howard's newspaper, the way that a criminal court bailiff might clip references to a notorious murder case before allowing the afternoon paper into the jury room.

Once he's bought a book, it's too late. "But do you actually think you're going to read *A Time to Heal* by Gerald Ford?" I asked one spring, in the slim hope that I could persuade him to include it in a couple of boxes of books I was about to take down to the local Veterans Administration hospital.

"Not now, of course," he said. "It's the sort of book you save for the summer."

I've never known what else to do except to encourage him in his carpentry, if that's what it is, on the theory that if he believes it's a worthwhile activity he might feel less guilty about not completing what he seems to treat as the homework the publishing industry has assigned all citizens. I haven't had the nerve to suggest to Edna that she do the same; she once confessed to me that if Howard presented her with one more useless and outlandish piece of furniture she might attempt to turn him into a lawn chair and donate him to the Salvation Army.

"That's a fine-looking firewood box you've made over there out of old baker's tins," I said when Howard was carrying on about the Stockman book.

"It's a telephone caddy," Howard said glumly.

"Well, it's a very handsome piece anyway," I said. "I think there's something quite artistic about that jagged edge in the back there."

"I don't suppose you've read *Caveat: Realism, Reagan, and Foreign Policy* by Alexander Haig, have you?" Howard asked.

"Howard, you know I don't read political memoirs," I said. "I don't mind listening to what politicians say when they're in office, but I'm certainly not going to pay to hear it all over again."

"I thought I should read it as another foreign policy view if I read *The Real War* by Richard Nixon," Howard said.

"Did you read *The Real War* by Richard Nixon?"

"No, it's over there behind *The Vantage Point* by Lyndon Johnson," Howard said. "I feel terrible about that. What a waste! What a terrible waste!"

I paid another visit to the Corkums' a few weeks later, expecting to find Howard sunk even deeper in his summer swamp of guilt. Instead I found him whistling cheerfully.

Flunking the Test

May 25, 1986

YOU MIGHT AS WELL KNOW that the increasing use of psychological testing in hiring has me worried. You probably think that what I'm worried about is some profound issue of public policy — the potential threat to employee privacy, maybe, or the possibility of civil liberties being eroded. It's nothing like that. What worries me about these tests is the realization that I couldn't pass one.

You might as well know that I can't draw hands. There! I've said it! It's something I've been keeping inside myself for years. I can hear you saying, "What's the big deal?" That's easy for you to say. You can probably draw hands.

I think I'd better start from the beginning. I have to go back to the days when I was in college. I know that when people start talking about things that they've kept inside themselves for years they're supposed to go back to their infancy, but, unfortunately, I've never been able to remember my infancy.

In fact, I tend to be a little hazy about anything that happened before I graduated from high school. As long as we're talking about it, you might as well know that I don't always have an absolutely firm grasp on events that took place, say, last week. Just today, for instance, I realized that I can't remember where I hid the good brandy last week in the course of preparing for a visit from my sweet old Uncle Herman.

I wouldn't admit that on a psychological test, of course. I wouldn't admit that I hid the good brandy from my sweet old Uncle Herman ("Prospective employee shows indications of devious behavior") and I wouldn't admit that I couldn't remember where I hid it ("Prospective employee shows signs of extreme fogginess"). You might as well know that I'd fail anyway: I can't draw hands.

While I was in college, I had a chance to get a summer job in an air-conditioned office, but it required completing a psychological test that had to be sent in with the application. Until the hands-drawing came up, I was doing pretty well. The first question, as I remember it, was something like this: If you found out that a fellow worker who had use of a company car was making a six-block detour every day to take his little girl to nursery school, would you (1) pretend you hadn't found out, (2) ask him if he would mind picking up a pack of cigarettes for you on the way back, or (3) upbraid him for abusing the trust of his employers, turn him in immediately to the appropriate manager, and possibly beat him about the head and shoulders with a riding crop. I knew what to say. They could count on me.

There were a few more questions like that. I was feeling pretty confident. Then I turned the page. I came upon a page that was nearly blank. At the top there was a single instruction: "Draw a man." I froze. Just after the instruction, within parentheses, it said that skill in drawing was not relevant. I knew that to be a simple lie.

I could see the test analyzers sitting around making fun of my drawing: "Hey, Harry, will you get a load of this one? Is that the guy's head or is he about to get hit by a basketball or what?"

Still, the alternative to this summer job was a job as a construction laborer in Kansas City. It's very hot in Kansas City in the summer. So I practiced drawing a man. As it happened, I've always been able to draw a man better than I'm able to draw most things, although I'll admit that a roommate who happened to glance at my desk while I was practicing asked why I was doing a picture of a picnic table.

Finally, I managed to draw what I thought was a pretty good picture of a man, except for one problem: I couldn't draw the hands. I solved that problem in the usual way. I drew a picture of a man with his hands in his pockets.

Just from having taken Introductory Psychology 201, I could see what was going to happen when the analyzers saw my man: "Prospective employee is trying to look cool. Prospective employee apparently has guilt complex that causes him to hide what he believes to be dirt on his hands. Prospective employee is a klutz who can't draw hands."

I tried putting his hands behind his back. That made it look as if he had just had both arms broken by a mob enforcer. I tried covering his hands with mittens. But I couldn't do an overcoat, so he looked like a man who for some reason wore mittens indoors. ("Prospective employee has a morbid fear of cold fingers.")

Finally, I decided to take the construction job in Kansas City. At first I worried constantly that the foreman would point at me and say, "O.K., you. We need someone up on the roof who can draw hands, and make it snappy." But he never did. After a while, I managed to think I had forgotten about not being able to draw hands. Until now. I'm glad it's all out.

My Life in Poetry

June 1, 1986

WHEN THE POWERS-THAT-BE in Washington finally decided that the United States should have a poet laureate, a sort of designated versifier, Robert Penn Warren was the obvious choice. He's so gifted that he would have become a renowned literary figure even if he had made the mistake, back at the beginning of his career, of signing his work plain Bob Warren.

If he had done that, of course, it might have taken him a lot longer to become recognized. People would have said, "Hey, I liked that novel about that governor in Louisiana by whatzisname. Bill Warren?"

"No, Bill Warren's the guy down at the bank."

"Maybe Bob Warren."

"There's a Bob Warren Pontiac out on old Highway 50, and wasn't there a Bob Warren used to pitch relief for the Cardinals?"

"Well, anyway, it was a good book by some guy."

I was so pleased by Warren's selection that I wrote a little poem in his honor:

Who has poetic gifts scarcer than the tooth of a hen?
Robert Penn.

Yes, I write poems now and then. I just thought I'd mention that in passing. As long as we're on the subject, though, I just thought I'd also mention that in the United States the poet laureate only serves for a one- or two-year term, and since there's nobody quite as obvious as Robert Penn Warren in the wings, the next term is up for grabs. I just thought I'd mention that.

To deal with the obvious question right off the bat: there's no reason to believe that having published a lot of poems is a prerequisite for holding this office. I'd make that point if, by chance, I happened to appear before whichever crowd in Washington decides who should be the next poet laureate — or, in these liberated times, the next poetess laureatette. I see it as a blue-ribbon commission made up of the Librarian of Congress and some senator who has demonstrated a flair for simile ("just as happy as a hog in slop") and a particularly literate Supreme Court justice and maybe a savings-and-loan lobbyist or two.

Acknowledging that they were not terribly familiar with my work, they'd ask me if I had written any poems lately that I was particularly proud of, and I would mention a poignant sonnet I did not long ago about a fish-smoker who dreams of becoming a country music singer.

"Is that a fairly common situation?" the Supreme Court justice says, sounding a bit puzzled.

"Let's hear the man out," says the senator, who, I happen to know, comes from a fish-smoking state.

I recite the poem:

Smoking fish just ain't my dish. I want to be a star.
I want to sing some lonesome country ballads,
Not smoke this fish for people's salads.
I've got some country stories I could tell.
In a roadside dump this country cracker'll
Be better off than smoking mackerel.
I've got to leave this awful fishy smell.
Smoking fish just ain't my dish. I want to be a star.

They're obviously impressed. I think I notice tears in the eyes of the senator from the fish-smoking state. The justice wants to know whether I've ever written on public issues, so I recite the poem I wrote about the national scandal of people performing mime on our streets:

Nobody really likes mime.
Nobody knows what they're showing.
Boat rowing? Lawn mowing? Grass growing?
If he's paying somebody a peso
To make him some chili con queso,
Couldn't he simply just say so?
A few words would help — can't they see?
What could the cost to them be?
Speech in this country is free!
Nobody knows what they're playing.
Spring haying? Croqueting? Egg laying?
There's really no reason or rhyme.
Nobody really likes mime.

The panelists are nodding. The Supreme Court justice says, "I like that part about free speech." I thought he might. The lobbyists ask if I'd like some campaign funds. I tell them that I'm not running for office. They ask me if I'd like some campaign funds anyway. I know then that I'm probably in.

The rest of the panelists look at the Librarian of Congress. He consults a print-out of names on the desk in front of him. Then he gives the all-clear sign: I've got no books overdue. It's done. I write a little poem in celebration:

> Who is now the poet laureate of the United States
>   even though his poems might have been rejected
>   by editors from sea to shining sea?
> Me.

Social Notes from
Aunt Rosie

June 8, 1986

MY AUNT ROSIE called from Kansas City to ask me who was at the luncheon that Reinaldo and Carolina Herrera gave at Mortimer's for the Rajmata of Jaipur.

"Is this a bad connection, Aunt Rosie," I said, "or have you been trying out the pink catawba wine again?"

"Don't get smart with me, big shot," Aunt Rosie said. "I knew you when you could have been called the Diaper of Jaipur."

Whenever she calls me "big shot," it's clear that I'm in for trouble. Aunt Rosie takes it for granted that absolutely anybody who lives in New York is clued in about all sorts of sophisticated matters that remain mysterious to what she calls the "meatloaf crowd" at home, and she is horrified anew every time I prove to know less about such things than she does. On one hand, she assumes that I'm personally acquainted with every glitz-hound who has ever been mentioned in the gossip columns; on the other hand, she's constantly complaining that the only one of her nephews who moved to New York is so completely without connections that he can't even get an out-of-town relative tickets to *Cats*.

"Aunt Rosie," I said, "I wasn't even aware that Reinaldo and Carolina Herrera were acquainted with the Rajmata of Jaipur. How in the world would you know that these people had lunch at Snerd's?"

"Not Snerd's, dummy. Mortimer's," Aunt Rosie said. "And I know it because I read it in *Vanity Fair*."

My heart sank. A couple of years ago, Aunt Rosie and her bridge friends started reading tony magazines like *Architectural Digest* and *House & Garden* and *European Travel & Life* — the sort of magazines that, according to a rather sour friend of mine known as Marty Mean Tongue, are someday going to be made into a composite television show called *Lifestyles of the Rich and Useless*. Aunt Rosie started calling me with questions like, "Listen, how much do you figure the Baroness de Gelt had to fork over for that chateau they showed in the November issue?" and "Hey, what kind of bucks are we talking about for a yard of that fabric the Countess used on her sun porch in Capri?"

I know how these questions must come about. Aunt Rosie and her bridge pals — the people she always calls the Jell-O Mold Rangers — leaf through these magazines, mainly to speculate on how much everything costs. Then, when the speculation deteriorates into a heated disagreement, Aunt Rosie says, "I'll just call my nephew who lives in New York. He'll be able to tell us, even though he's a little slow."

Now the Jell-O Mold Rangers had obviously taken to

reading *Vanity Fair.* It was bad enough answering questions about how much I figured some cat-food heiress had
to pay a yard for the chintz on her couches. Now I was
going to get constant questions about the parties given by
dress designers and charity-ball trotters and New Jersey
countesses and what Marty Mean Tongue always calls the
Von de Von crowd — people whose social activities *Vanity
Fair* chronicles so devotedly that Marty refers to it as the
house organ of the Eurotrash.

Apparently, the *Vanity Fair* coverage of the Rajmata's
luncheon presented a seating chart of the table with first
names only and challenged the reader to guess the full
name. "I know who C.Z. is, of course, because I saw her
patio in *Architectural Digest* or somewhere," Aunt Rosie
said. "And Pat is obvious: she had Oscar's dress on when
she was talking to Jerome a couple of issues ago. But who
do you think Tom is? I told Myrtle Weber you'd know for
sure."

"I don't suppose Tom could be Tom Beasley, Cousin
Bernie's partner in the laundromat," I said. "That Tom
certainly could be counted on to show up at a free lunch."

"I don't know what made me think you'd know," Aunt
Rosie said. "I always told your mother you'd never amount
to anything."

"I guess it's unlikely that an Indian princess would be
interested in meeting a country singer like Tom T. Hall,"
I said. "Unless maybe he's added an amplified sitar to his
back-up group."

There was a long silence. Then Aunt Rosie said, "Myrtle
Weber's son in New York said he could get us tickets to
Cats anytime we wanted them."

"I'm sure he can," I said. "Taxi drivers are surprisingly

good at that sort of thing. I read a story about it in the *New York Times* — a publication, I should mention, that you and the Jell-O Mold Rangers might think of reading instead of these glossy gossip sheets you seem to favor."

"I already take the *Times*," Aunt Rosie said. "For that Evening Hours column they have. That's how I knew who the Lee was that Reinaldo and Carolina seated next to C.Z. and why Estée was put next to Bob."

"Is it because Bob tends to spill things late in the meal?" I said.

"Listen, I knew you when the only Indian princess you had ever heard of was Pocahontas," Aunt Rosie said. "So save your smart-aleck talk for your fancy New York friends, big shot."

Invitation from Mrs. T.

June 16, 1986

AS IT BECAME CLEAR that Americans' fear of terrorism was having a dismal effect on the British tourist industry, I was pleased to read in the paper that we'd all been invited back to England this summer by Margaret Thatcher herself. But my old Army buddy Charlie says he's not going anywhere until he gets a personal apology for the Sussex stationery-shop incident.

"I don't think that's very likely, Charlie," I said, "considering all the damage you did to the shop."

"Also, I want an apology for that thing in Barnstaple," Charlie said. "And all that court business."

"Mrs. Thatcher says it's not just that they're worried about the effect on the economy now that American tourism's way down," I reminded Charlie. "She says she misses our friendliness."

"Well, I sure don't miss their friendliness a whole lot," Charlie said. "Especially that bunch of little bitty foreigners that jumped me in Barnstaple that time."

"Are you, by chance, referring to the Barnstaple police department, Charlie?" I said.

"Well, whoever," he said.

I'll admit to being a little surprised that Charlie has been invited back to England. He's never been invited back to anywhere else. It's true that just before his trip over there, I tried to prepare him for some of the cultural differences that exist between the English and what Charlie insists on calling "regular people." Charlie, after all, had never been out of the country except for the Mexican trip that ended with what he calls "that little difference of opinion in Ensenada."

I can't say, though, that the preparation showed any signs of doing much good. When I told him that the English still drive on the left-hand side of the road, for instance, he said that he thought any country that did that ought to lose its vote in the United Nations.

I explained a few other differences — that the English like to say "thank you," even if you happen to have just said "thank you" to them, for instance, and that they seem to enjoy standing quietly in orderly lines. Charlie thought about that for a while and then said, "What it sounds like to me is that they're kind of weird."

"Well, they're used to a different way of doing things, Charlie," I said. "For instance, I don't think London's really a perfect place for your traditional water-bomb barrage on the first night at the hotel."

I'll admit that before Charlie went over there I was also rather concerned about how the English might react to the sheer size of him. When we were in the Army, Charlie was thought of as pretty big, and he has steadily grown bigger. He reminds me of a serious eater I know who moved from the East to New Orleans and later told me, "As much as I like the food down here, I only gain about five pounds a year; the trouble is, I've lived here for nine years."

The effect of Charlie's size is compounded by his tendency to travel in his favorite Jayhawk sweatshirt — symbolic of the semester and a half he put in at the University of Kansas before what he always refers to as "the little trouble down at the Tri-Delt house." The sweatshirt, in bright red, isn't the sort of sweatshirt that simply says KANSAS JAYHAWKS on it; it's designed to look like a jayhawk, with two huge eyes around chest level and a ferocious-looking beak resting almost horizontally on Charlie's stomach. It occurred to me that a British immigration officer who saw Charlie lumbering toward him in a Jayhawk sweatshirt, chanting the Rawk-Chalk Jayhawk cheer that Charlie uses as a sort of marching song, might get the impression that he was about to be run over by the point man in an invasion from outer space.

Who could have predicted that Charlie would be invited back by the Prime Minister? Who could have predicted that he would refuse to return unless she apologized personally for the incident that began when the immigration officer responded to Charlie's approach by calling for reinforcements?

"Charlie," I said, "it seems unrealistic to expect the Prime Minister of the entire country to call you personally to apologize, particularly considering the number of policemen who were injured at the airport."

"I don't see why," Charlie said. "All those court papers said right on them that they were from the Queen of the whole country. Also, those people tore my sweatshirt. One of the eyes still looks a little funny."

"I think Mrs. Thatcher was really being sincere,

Charlie," I said. "She said she loves our warmth and generosity."

"Those are a couple of things she could use a little of herself," Charlie said. "A warm and generous person would admit when she made a mistake by prosecuting for some tiny little misunderstanding."

"Well, she just wants us all to know that the English miss us," I said.

"I miss them too; they're a hoot," Charlie said. "I swear — some of those folks acted like they'd never seen a water bomb before. Maybe I'll go back the summer after this. But they're going to have to watch their manners between now and then."

Not Hiring Deaver

June 22, 1986

WE'VE DECIDED not to hire Michael J. Deaver as our Washington lobbyist.

We are an organization of people who have to travel constantly in our jobs — traveling salesmen, reporters, regional auditors, people who cross state lines to advocate the overthrow of the government by force and violence, IRS examiners, itinerant confidence men.

We are the American Association of Traveling People, known as AATP. We realize that as an acronym AATP is difficult to pronounce. That's intentional: while you're trying to figure out how to pronounce it, we sneak ahead of you in the rental car line.

We have any number of problems, but there's no doubt about which item is at the top of our Washington want-list: a presidential order stating that any city that does not have the route to its airport clearly marked shall lose all of its major league franchises.

A year or so ago, when it was announced that Michael J. Deaver was about to set up a lobbying firm, we had a meeting to consider hiring him as our lobbyist. He had, after all, become one of the three most powerful people in the White House — an impressive achievement for someone whose most serious talents were said to lie in the direction of knowing precisely which camera angle was most flattering to each of Nancy Reagan's ball gowns. He is so close to Ronald and Nancy Reagan that he is often described as being like a son to them — something that has never been said of any of their own children.

One of our board members — Larry Green, a traveler in mid-priced ladies' sportswear — did bring up a few incidents that had led him to believe Deaver has what Larry referred to as "an ethical blind spot in both eyes."

Larry reminded us that Deaver had once recommended for a job on the Postal Service Board of Governors someone who had just arranged a large loan for him. In Reagan's first term, Larry said, only a public uproar prevented Deaver from going through with plans for publishing a diet book while he was serving as the deputy chief of staff of the White House. (The first week's menu in *The Reagan White House Diet Book*, I suppose, would simply tell you to live on what's now offered in the school lunch program. Then you'd spend the next week eating as if you were a pensioner faced with the cutbacks in the food stamp program. You've lost fourteen pounds.)

Larry reminded me that I myself had once offered as a theory on how Ronald Reagan got scheduled to visit Bitburg Cemetery in the first place the possibility that Micheal Deaver, who was advance man for the trip, had no time to find out if there happened to be any S.S. troops buried there because he was too busy choosing extras for the BMW he arranged to buy at diplomat's discount with his temporary diplomatic passport.

I reminded Larry that the man in charge of maintaining ethical standards at the White House — a man who these days must feel a bit like the high school history teacher who has been designated to enforce the no-drinking rule at the all-night graduation party — cleared Deaver on the BMW deal with one of those "Never Been Indicted" endorsements. Also, I told Larry that maybe he was being too strict, holding someone in the White House to the ethical standards of the dress business.

Larry got desperate enough to come around to my way of thinking one day while he was racing for the last plane out of some city in Ohio: he somehow managed to follow a bewildering hodgepodge of signs to Buzz Landon Memorial Field, arriving ten minutes before the flight to discover that Buzz Landon Memorial Field was the sort of field upon which small boys play Little League baseball.

We were about to approach Deaver when the controversy erupted about whether, in lobbying on such issues as acid rain, he had broken the law prohibiting government employees from lobbying for a year on any issue with which they have been "personally and substantially" involved. I was for hiring him anyway. Every time I thought of poor Larry Green screeching to a stop in front of Landon Field just in time to see a nine-year-old shortstop juggle a grounder, I realized anew that these are desperate times.

Then Deaver began defending himself. First he said that he would never exploit his relationship with the Reagans — the very relationship we were going to hire him to exploit. Then he made what amounted to a claim that he hadn't been involved substantially with issues like acid rain because he had never been involved substantially with anything — a claim the lawyers must call the Lightweight Defense. He said that he still doesn't understand what acid rain is.

Larry saw that quote and put his foot down. "If he doesn't understand what acid rain is, he'll never understand what it's like to try finding the rental car drop-off place when the arrow seems to point to long-term parking," he said.

We called an extraordinary session of the board, asking all the members to come to Washington from wherever they were at the end of the week so that we could interview other lobbyists. Unfortunately, only two board members showed up. The rest got lost on the way to the airport.

Oreos to the Moon

June 29, 1986

I DON'T KNOW about anybody else, but I found it a bit disquieting to learn that if all of the Oreo cookies made in the past seventy-five years were stacked on top of one another, they would go to the moon and back four times.

The problem, I think, was that I heard about it on the radio one morning while I was preoccupied with trying to get some breakfast on the table for my daughters. I was rummaging around in the refrigerator looking for the orange juice, so I wasn't paying absolutely perfect attention. I don't suppose I could have heard absolutely perfectly even if I had been paying attention, what with my head halfway inside the refrigerator and one ear up against some lettuce that probably should have been thrown out a couple of days before. Somehow, I managed to get the impression that as part of the celebration of the seventy-fifth anniversary of Oreo cookies, these Oreo stacks to the moon were actually in the process of being completed.

Of course I realized sooner or later that my interpretation didn't make sense. In the first place, it's obvious that most of the Oreos sold over the last seventy-five years are unavailable for stacking. It's not likely, after all, that the people who bought them kept them around just on the off chance that someone might come along who wanted to stack them to the moon and back four times. Those Oreos are eaten up. Also, it seems doubtful that the technology is available to stack Oreos to the moon even once, although you'd be surprised what some of those promotion people can accomplish once they get up a head of steam.

Although I have the reputation of not being completely tuned in on technological matters — a reputation that I trace back to the day several years ago when I threw the electric can opener out the window — even I can see some technological questions that would have to be answered before launching an attempt to stack Oreo cookies to the moon. Would you have to use some kind of glue to hold the cookies together, for instance, or could you just put an extra smear of cream filling between cookies? What sort of ladder would you stand on? Would you need to know how to operate an electric can opener?

I don't mean to imply that I couldn't see any good in the project at all. For one thing, I figured that it might be a way of freshening up that tired phrase about how various national problems should be soluble for a country that put a man on the moon. People could start saying, "You can't tell me that a nation that can create eight Oreo stacks to the moon — four up and four back — isn't able to find a cure for the common cold."

Still, after that first flash of thinking about Oreo stacks to the moon as a real possibility, I began to feel uneasy as similar claims from the manufacturers of other foodstuffs drifted into my mind. A few years ago, for instance, I read that if all the Kentucky Fried chickens sold by 1980 were placed end to end they'd stretch for ninety-three thousand miles, which is almost four times around the world, assuming you didn't have to make any detours because of running into a string of Whopper Burgers that the Burger King folks had strung back and forth between the North and South Poles.

All day, I caught myself glancing out the window toward the horizon now and then, just on the off chance I'd see a line of fifty-five billion McDonald's hamburgers on its way to someplace like Saturn and back.

I suppose I must have still had it on my mind when I went to sleep at night, because I immediately started dreaming of Soviet cosmonauts talking to their mission control people in Russian (a language I ordinarily don't understand) about what to do to avoid a figure eight of Good Humor bars that seemed to be in the path of their spaceship's orbit. According to what a television newscaster was saying, a mountain of Hershey bars the size of West Virginia had been placed too close to the equator and was threatening to melt, with grave implications for the neighboring country of Gambia.

Somehow, the radio was on at the same time. I thought I heard the radio announcer say that Australia had disappeared ("From the information available now, it appears that the Coca-Cola people tried to demonstrate that all the Coke drunk over the past one hundred years could fill the basin of the Pacific Ocean, and there wasn't really room for two oceans in there"). The planet would have to be evacuated. People were already fleeing to the moon, inching their way slowly up a stack of Oreos.

My Team

BENNO SCHMIDT, JR., the new president of Yale, has been described in the press as a "renowned constitutional-law scholar who is an expert on the First Amendment, race relations, and the New York Rangers." The man he will replace, A. Bartlett Giamatti, has been described as "a professor of English and comparative literature and an expert on Dante, Spenser, and the Boston Red Sox." It's no wonder I'm never asked to be the president of a major educational institution: I don't have a team.

I used to have a team. When I was growing up, the Kansas City Blues were my team. They were in the American Association, along with the Minneapolis Millers and the Milwaukee Brewers and the Toledo Mud Hens (the league patsies) and several other teams that Schmidt and Giamatti don't know the first thing about.

Because I grew up in Kansas City, people assume that the Kansas City Royals are my team. Not so. My loyalty to the Kansas City Blues was so pure that their demise ended my interest in the national pastime. Oh sure, I could have skipped to the Kansas City Athletics and then to the Royals. I had opportunities. "It's the big leagues," everyone in Kansas City said when the Athletics came in to replace the Blues.

"Big leaguers don't ditch their pals," I replied.

I could see myself running into one of the old Kansas City Blues someday — Cliff Mapes, maybe, or Eddie Stewart, or Carl DeRose, the sore-arm right-hander I once saw pitch a perfect game. Or maybe Odie Strain, the no-hit shortstop. "I guess you follow the Royals now," Odie would say, with that same look of resignation he used to wear when the third strike whisked past him and thwocked into the catcher's mitt.

"No," I'd say. "I don't have a team. My team's gone." A smile would spread slowly across Odie's face.

Meanwhile, I don't have a team. I can just imagine my appearance before the presidential search committee of, say, the Harvard trustees. I'm being interviewed in a private room at the New York Harvard Club by a former secretary of defense, an enormously wealthy investment banker, and an Episcopalian bishop. So far, I feel that things have been going my way. I have analyzed Dante's *Divine Comedy* in constitutional terms, concentrating on whether moaning in purgatory is a First Amendment–protected right. I have transposed the first ten amendments to the Constitution into Spenserian stanzas, although not in a pushy way.

I can see that the committee is impressed. The former secretary of defense, who at first seemed to be concentrating on some doodling that resembled the trajectory of an intercontinental ballistic missile, is now giving the interview his complete attention. The investment banker has slipped me a note that says, "Hold on to Humboldt Bolt & Tube. Sell Worldwide Universal short." The interviewers are exchanging pleased glances and nodding their heads. Finally, as the interview seems to be coming to an end, the investment banker says, "Just one more question. What is your team?"

"Team?" I say.

There is a long silence. Then the bishop in a kindly voice says, "You do have a team, don't you?"

"Well, not exactly," I say.

"No team?" the bishop says.

"I used to have a team," I say, "and I still turn on the tennis now and then, just to hiss McEnroe."

The bishop shakes his head sadly.

I am beginning to get desperate. "I know the University of Missouri fight song by heart," I say.

But they are gathering up their papers, preparing to leave. The former defense secretary is carefully feeding his doodles into a paper shredder.

"But why do I need a team?" I say.

Nobody pays any attention except the bishop, who says, "We need a regular guy. Presidents who aren't regular guys frighten the alumni."

"But I *am* a regular guy," I say. "I owe the Diners Club. I had a dog named Spike."

"Regular guys have teams," the bishop says.

Desperately, I begin to sing: "Every true son so happy hearted, skies above us are blue. There's a spirit so deep within us. Old Missouri, here's to you — rah, rah. When the band plays the Tiger . . ."

But now they are at the door. Suddenly the investment banker walks back to where I'm sitting, snatches his stock tips off the table, and marches out with the rest of the committee. I sit stunned at the table as a club steward comes in to straighten up the room. He glances down at my résumé, still on the table.

"Kansas City, huh?" he says. "You must be proud of those Royals."

"The Royals are not my team," I say. "I don't have a team. If I had a team, I'd be the president of Harvard."

Calories May Not Count

July 13, 1986

YOU'VE PROBABLY BEEN wondering how they figure out just how many calories there are in, say, a four-ounce Italian sausage. I've been wondering the same thing. You may have been wondering about it for the same reason I've been wondering about it: maybe they're wrong. Maybe calculating calories is a science that is about as exact as handicapping horses.

Let's consider a liberating possibility: maybe a scoop of low-fat cottage cheese decorated with fresh orange slices has just as many calories as a four-ounce Italian sausage. Let's consider an even more liberating possibility: maybe a scoop of low-fat cottage cheese decorated with fresh orange slices has just as many calories as a four-ounce Italian sausage on a roll with fried onions and peppers, plus a couple of cans of beer. Now we're getting somewhere.

My wife says that they're absolutely right about how many calories are in a four-ounce Italian sausage. But how can she be certain? I keep reminding her that a healthy skepticism is an essential of scientific inquiry. Galileo did not simply accept the court astronomers' explanation of why the sun revolved around the earth ("The earth couldn't move because of the weight of Italian sausage"). Newton did not simply accept the conventional explanation of why a dropped piece of Italian sausage fell down rather than up ("Otherwise, it would keep flying out of the roll").

Lately, I've been reminding my wife that when William Geist of the *New York Times* went looking some time ago for the Fashion Foundation of America, an organization that has for years been issuing a widely publicized list of the best-dressed men in America, he found that it amounted to a single old press agent in a one-room office in Brooklyn.

Here we've been accepting the best-dressed list all these years as if it were the scientific findings of an expert panel that went around calibrating people's lapels and testing the sharpness of their trouser creases against day-old bread and checking the lumps in their jacket pockets for Italian sausage sandwiches. Here my wife has for years been saying things like, "Maybe if you'd dress a little more like Cesar Romero, you'd be on the Fashion Foundation of America's list of best-dressed men yourself" — or thinking such things, at least, when she said something like, "You're not really going to go out of the house wearing that jacket, are you?"

"Maybe the calorie counts come from some outfit that has a fancy name like the National Caloric Census Council but amounts to a couple of ex-vaudeville hoofers with a one-room office in Buffalo," I said to my wife.

"Don't be silly," she said. "It's done in a laboratory."

That, I might just point out, is precisely what she said last year when I asked her what sort of tweezers they could possibly use to extract the caffeine from coffee beans for de-caf coffee.

In fact, I don't see the de-caf operation taking place in a laboratory. I imagine a building that looks like a gigantic tobacco shed. Dozens of caffeine extractors are sitting at long tables, picking away with their tiny, weirdly shaped tweezers. But what do they do with the caffeine they extract? Is it just piled in heaps around Central American villages, like so much coal slag? If so, isn't there a danger that village dogs might sniff around the heaps and end up being wide awake for a year and half?

In other words, there's no reason to assume that this calorie-counting is done in a laboratory. I see the Buffalo operation in an ordinary, rather shabby office that used to be the headquarters of the Western New York Accordion Association. The two ex-hoofers who run it have no scientific experience beyond whatever physics is required to judge the velocity of a rotten tomato thrown from the tenth row. They're often out of tweezers.

"I have the dictionary right here," said my wife, who knows how to put a damper on a scientific discussion. "It says a calorie is the quantity of energy required to raise a thousand grams of water one degree centigrade."

"Exactly my point!" I said.

I can see the Buffalo guys heating up the Italian sausage to see how much it will raise the temperature of an old coffeepot full of water. "Jeez, that smells good, Harry," one of them says. "Why don't we toss in some onions and peppers."

By the time they're eating their Italian sausage sandwiches, the water has been forgotten. "This stuff must be worth a thousand easy," Harry says, smacking his lips.

"Call it fifteen hundred," his partner says, "and pass the beer."

The Correct Change

July 20, 1986

A PRESIDENTIAL COMMISSION has been appointed to inquire into why stewardesses who sell drinks on airplanes never carry any change. I am the chairman. Why shouldn't I be the chairman? I'm the guy who's been sitting there all these years with his stewardess call button on, waiting nervously for the change from his ten-dollar bill. I'm the guy who keeps asking stewardesses why they don't carry change, only to be told to fasten my seat belt and return my tray table and seat back to their original upright positions.

I'll accept the job with the understanding that I'll have total independence from the Administration. Before I've even had a chance to appoint my staff, though, the attorney general, in a speech to a black-tie gathering of assorted California wackos, says that it is important not to deviate from the intentions of the Founding Fathers on the issue of exact change. Then one of the White House economic advisers, a man who spends most of his time testing his theory that the budget deficit can be reduced by sticking pins into a tiny effigy of the national debt, says that attempting to regulate the amount of change anyone carries would constitute governmental interference in private enterprise.

I could, of course, remind the attorney general that the only indication we have of how the Founding Fathers felt about anything relating to this issue is Benjamin Franklin's pre-Revolutionary comment that King George III's tax officials were "nickel-and-diming us to death." I could point out to the White House economic adviser that his pin-sticking rituals will have no effect because the effigy he's using looks nothing like the national debt. (The national debt is, in fact, a purple blob, somewhat larger at one end.)

That is not what I do. What I do is go straight to the White House. I walk into the Oval Office. "With all respect, Mr. President," I say, "tell your gunsels to lay off, or find yourself another boy."

With that matter settled, I begin choosing the members of my commission. I invite the president of the Airline Passengers Organization, but he says he will serve only if he is given ten thousand frequent-flier miles on his Pan Am World Pass, fourteen upgrades through the American Advantage program, and a free weekend for two at the Sheraton of his choice. I make a counteroffer of an all-airline thirty-day pass that allows you to fly anywhere in the continental United States as long as it's raining there. He jumps at it.

I also appoint Leon W. Grentham, Professor of Small Change at Harvard Business School, who did the breakthrough calculations showing that if a megacorporation in the retail trades instructed its cashiers to make change so slowly that some customers got tired of waiting and went home, it could make up to $7 million a day on the float.

Then I appoint Rod Burlington, director of a notoriously tough urban survival training school whose final examination consists of dropping the trainee into midtown Manhattan with nothing but a quarter and graduating him only if he manages to persuade someone to change it for two dimes and a nickel.

Once the word gets out that I am the chairman of the commission, a number of theories come to my attention.

"Stewardesses hate airline passengers because the passengers keep saying 'stewardess' instead of 'flight attendant' and 'airplane' instead of 'aircraft,' " one citizen writes. "They aren't allowed to display their hatred openly, so they get back at the passengers by not carrying any change and by hiding all magazines except *Jack and Jill.*"

We hold hearings. The first witness is the president of the Flight Attendants Association.

"Why don't you people ever carry change?" I ask.

"I'll look in the back, sir," she says. "I thought we had some with the pillows."

"The question was why you don't carry change," I say rather sternly.

"Could you please just fasten your seat belt, sir," she says. "We're coming into an area of turbulence."

"We're on the ground," I say. "This is a presidential commission. I'm the chairman."

"Perhaps you'd like a magazine, sir," she says, handing me a copy of *Jack and Jill.*

Out of habit, I start leafing through the magazine and find myself wondering whether there will be any traffic delay when we get to LaGuardia. Suddenly realizing where we are, I throw down the magazine and tell the witness she is excused. She shows no sign of leaving.

The commission's counsel whispers to me that we are obligated to reimburse the witness $5.50 for taxi fare.

"Here," I say, reaching into my wallet and handing her a ten-dollar bill. "Here's your cab fare."

"You don't happen to have the exact change, do you, sir?" she asks.

I don't. Desperately I look up and down the table at my fellow commission members. They look in their wallets. Then they shake their heads.

"I'll have to get back to you, sir," she says, taking the ten dollars. Before she leaves, she switches on my stewardess call button.

Design Disagreement

July 27, 1986

MY WIFE AND I HAD what you might call a little design disagreement — a difference of opinion about where to put the neon beer sign that my friend Morland gave me for my birthday. I thought the sign might look good shining out the living room window where it would cheer the neighbors, give the house a rather festive air, and provide a beacon for seamen in distress. My wife thought a good place for it might be the closet. These things happen.

Morland gave me the sign because ever since infancy I have shared a nickname with the beer it advertises. Not Schlitz. Even in Kansas City, nobody calls a baby Schlitz for short. We did have a perfectly rectangular little guard on our high school football team who was called Six-Pack Sawyer. As a rule, though, we stayed away from brand names; this beer and I shared a nickname by mere coincidence.

The sign says, in three colors of neon, THIS BUD's FOR YOU. It's gorgeous. Morland knew I'd appreciate it. He's got a special feel for that sort of thing — maybe because his friends from Toronto, where he grew up, often call him Moosehead.

I wasn't surprised that my wife and I had a little design disagreement over the sign. It wasn't our first. We had one several years ago over my four-by-six-foot American Hereford Association poster. Again the two positions seemed far apart at first blush. I wanted to put the poster on the wall above the mantel. She wanted to throw it out.

I pointed out that the American Hereford Association has its national headquarters in Kansas City. She pointed out that we live in New York. I pointed out that the bull on top of the American Hereford Association building — a huge bull whose heart and liver light up at night — is one of the landmarks of my hometown. She pointed out that she has never believed that the heart and liver light up at night.

I pointed out that I have never attacked the landmarks of her hometown. These design disagreements can get away from you if you're not careful.

We might have gone on in that vein for another four or five years if, by chance, the American Hereford Association hadn't put its building up for sale, causing some concern in Kansas City about what would become of the landmark bull.

I said I thought it would look splendid on top of our house — although, since we live in one of those New York brownstone neighborhoods where the Historic District people don't permit fiddling with one's facade, we might have to pretend it was there when we moved in. My wife said that the bull was almost exactly the size of our house. That, I said, could be seen as a nice coincidence. Finally, she said, "Maybe it would be enough of a tribute to Herefords if we put up the American Hereford Association poster, in the hall." Marriage, as they say, is compromise.

There have been other design disagreements since — the disagreement over the foot-powder billboard, for instance, and the disagreement over the heroic lawn statue of a basset hound at bay. (No, not baying; at bay.) You win a few and you lose a few.

Still, I was particularly keen on that beer sign. I told my wife that for all we knew, Morland might have risked jail to get that sign. She told me that considering the sort of gifts Morland is in the habit of handing out, if he ever goes to jail it will be for littering.

She did agree that it would be only decent to display the sign when Morland came over for my birthday dinner. I put it on a prominent shelf between the kitchen windows — strategically placed so that someone sitting in certain parts of the living room could read by its light. Morland seemed pleased. When I pulled him aside to tell him that there was a little design disagreement that might make it difficult to keep the sign on the shelf, he told me that I had been using the wrong approach.

I should always use arguments based on aesthetics, he said, because that countered the unspoken belief of all women that their husbands are tasteless oafs. Morland has a lot of experience in these matters: he's been married five times.

As soon as he had gone, I tried one of the phrases he'd suggested. "Did you notice the way the sign picks up the horizontals of the window frames?" I said as we started doing the dishes.

My wife just looked at me oddly. At least she didn't say, "So would Six-Pack Sawyer."

"Also," I said, "the blue picks up that light blue from the living room carpet."

"What's all this 'picks up' talk?" my wife said. "You sound like that home-decorating hints brochure that comes free with the furniture polish."

I shrugged modestly. I wondered if I should go on to say that the curlicues of the neon script picked up some circular crayon marks one of the kids once drew on the kitchen wall.

My wife sighed. "Listen," she said. "I don't mind keeping the sign where it is, but I don't want to hear any more about what picks up what unless it's you picking up the garbage and taking it out to be emptied."

I snatched up the garbage can. "It *is* getting rather full," I said. My sign looked gorgeous. Marriage, as they say, is compromise.

Reagan Is Told
of Norwegian
Whaling Infractions

August 3, 1986

THE NEWSPAPER HEADLINE I've had on my bulletin board since early this summer says REAGAN IS TOLD OF NORWEGIAN WHALING INFRACTIONS. I didn't actually read the story that went with it. I seem to be doing more and more of that these days — saving the headline and not bothering to read the story. I sort of slipped into the habit, I suppose, when I began to realize that the stories weren't really measuring up.

It's almost certain, for instance, that what followed REAGAN IS TOLD OF NORWEGIAN WHALING INFRACTIONS — what I think of as the off-the-rack story — was a letdown. When the headline sounds that intriguing, I find that I prefer to keep it around and sort of customize some stories to go with it.

Of course, some headlines that are interesting in themselves aren't really suitable for custom-made stories. Several years ago, for instance, a friend of mine sent me a photocopy of a headline that said TWENTY-ONE MILLION AMERICANS HAVE NO TEETH AT ALL. I can't imagine where it came from. My friend has odd tastes; for all I know, he might subscribe to a weekly paper devoted to news of the denture industry.

I kept the headline on my bulletin board for a while, but I was never tempted to make up stories to go with it. It seemed to be a story in itself. I figured that my friend had sent it as a handy device for cheering me up anytime I was in a low mood. I think he wanted me to feel that when the cares of the world were too much with me — when I started worrying about the threat of the bomb and the age of my furnace and the damage being done by acid rain and the possibility that someday all movies will be Sylvester Stallone movies or Arnold Schwarzenegger movies — I could simply look at the headline on my bulletin board. Then I'd say, "Well, at least I have all my own teeth."

REAGAN IS TOLD OF NORWEGIAN WHALING INFRACTIONS, though, allows for any number of stories. For a while I thought of the story as a sort of gossip item written by one of those Washington reporters who specialize in making the rounds of diplomatic receptions and high-level dinner parties: "At a White House dinner last night, President Reagan made a graceful little after-dinner speech about the value of doing the right thing. He used as an example an American who finally decided to risk his life to help the Resistance during the Second World War — an American named Rick who operated a bar in Vichy-controlled Casablanca. The Norwegian ambassador to the United States was so moved that he confessed that he has been keeping a whale, the national animal of Norway, at his official residence in the Washington suburbs, in contravention of the animal control ordinances of Bethesda. The President told him not to give it another thought, and then went on to tell a story about how, in the days before bloated government had ensnarled the American people in red tape like animal control ordinances, a plucky little girl from the state of Kansas ignored complaints about her little dog, Toto — although both were later picked up by a tornado and blown away into a strange land."

Then I thought the headline might go with one of those human interest stories that often come out about the President: "Ronald Reagan, a storyteller of considerable reputation, admitted that he was one-upped yesterday during a ceremony honoring NATO fleet commanders. After the President told some stories about high jinks on the MGM lot in the forties, Admiral Lars Kulleseid of the Norwegian Royal Navy told of a prank during his naval cadet days: while the academy superintendent was away on a short trip, a dozen enterprising cadets managed to place a Beluga whale in his parlor. The President said, 'Well, that beats all.' "

Lately, though, it has occurred to me that the story might have more to do with the substantive issues of government. I see a meeting of some of the President's top advisers, right in the Oval Office. Pat Buchanan is talking to Donald Regan. "We've got to tell him something," Buchanan says, gesturing toward the President, who is sitting at his desk. "Why don't we tell him about the farm problem?"

"I hate to wake him up just for that," Regan says.

"He is awake," Ed Meese says. "I just saw him wink and grin and give the thumbs-up sign."

"Well, let's tell him about the deficit," James Baker says.

"You know he doesn't want to hear about the deficit," Regan says. "The last time I tried to bring it up he told me that story again about the welfare mother who picks up her check in a Cadillac. I think if he tells me that story one more time I'm going to defect."

"We've got to tell him something," Larry Speakes says. "I can't keep telling these reporters that the President is being briefed if we never tell him anything."

"Gentlemen," Buchanan says. "I think I've got it." He rummages around in the bottom of his briefcase, picks up a slim file, and walks to the President's desk. "Mr. President," he says, rather formally, "Norwegians have committed whaling infractions."

The President winks and grins and gives the thumbs-up sign.

Important Volumes

August 10, 1986

MY FRIEND HOWARD CORKUM took David Stockman's book to the cottage the Corkums have at the beach, and immediately started talking about how guilty he felt about not reading it.

"I feel terrible about this," Howard said when I went to visit them a few days after they opened up the cottage for the summer. "Here I've spent $22.95 for a book I haven't even opened. I can't imagine why I bought it in the first place. I mean, it's not as if I've been a big fan of David Stockman. He looks like he was George Will's roommate in college and they had the only absolutely tidy room in the dormitory."

"Take it easy, Howard," I said. "You just got here. How do you know you won't read it before the end of the summer?"

"That's how I know," Howard said, pointing to a small mountain of thick volumes on the other side of the parlor. I couldn't see all the titles from where I was sitting, but I did make out *Keeping Faith: Memoirs of a President* by

Jimmy Carter and *The White House Years* by Henry S. Kissinger. "I haven't opened any of them," Howard said. "I feel just awful about this whole thing."

None of this surprised me. Every winter, Howard, feverish with good intentions, buys some pound-and-a-half political memoir that he describes as "important," and puts it aside to read when he gets to the beach cottage in the summer. He never seems to remember that what he actually does at the beach all summer is putter around in an old shed turning found objects like driftwood and lobster buoys into small pieces of furniture that, in the words of the mutual friend we call Marty Mean Tongue, "make you understand that certain found objects were meant to remain lost."

Sitting there in the Corkums' parlor, wobbling slightly on a chair Howard has fashioned from railroad ties, I regretted not having thought to phone Howard's wife, Edna, last winter and suggest that she clip any mention of the Stockman book from Howard's newspaper, the way that a criminal court bailiff might clip references to a notorious murder case before allowing the afternoon paper into the jury room.

Once he's bought a book, it's too late. "But do you actually think you're going to read *A Time to Heal* by Gerald Ford?" I asked one spring, in the slim hope that I could persuade him to include it in a couple of boxes of books I was about to take down to the local Veterans Administration hospital.

"Not now, of course," he said. "It's the sort of book you save for the summer."

I've never known what else to do except to encourage him in his carpentry, if that's what it is, on the theory that if he believes it's a worthwhile activity he might feel less guilty about not completing what he seems to treat as the homework the publishing industry has assigned all citizens. I haven't had the nerve to suggest to Edna that she do the same; she once confessed to me that if Howard presented her with one more useless and outlandish piece of furniture she might attempt to turn him into a lawn chair and donate him to the Salvation Army.

"That's a fine-looking firewood box you've made over there out of old baker's tins," I said when Howard was carrying on about the Stockman book.

"It's a telephone caddy," Howard said glumly.

"Well, it's a very handsome piece anyway," I said. "I think there's something quite artistic about that jagged edge in the back there."

"I don't suppose you've read *Caveat: Realism, Reagan, and Foreign Policy* by Alexander Haig, have you?" Howard asked.

"Howard, you know I don't read political memoirs," I said. "I don't mind listening to what politicians say when they're in office, but I'm certainly not going to pay to hear it all over again."

"I thought I should read it as another foreign policy view if I read *The Real War* by Richard Nixon," Howard said.

"Did you read *The Real War* by Richard Nixon?"

"No, it's over there behind *The Vantage Point* by Lyndon Johnson," Howard said. "I feel terrible about that. What a waste! What a terrible waste!"

I paid another visit to the Corkums' a few weeks later, expecting to find Howard sunk even deeper in his summer swamp of guilt. Instead I found him whistling cheerfully.

Edna, it turned out, had made a decision. She had collected all of the political memoirs, lugged them to the shed, and informed Howard that what she really needed desperately was a stand to put next to the kitchen counter for the toaster and waffle iron.

Howard had gone for the idea at once. For a while he didn't think he had enough memoirs on hand, but then he found that he could fashion part of a leg from a number of James Michener novels Edna had been meaning to get to.

Naturally, I complimented him on the completed work.

"Well, it's not quite finished," Howard said. "When you get back to the city, I'd appreciate it if you could send me *No More Vietnams* by Richard Nixon. From what I understand about how long it is, it would be perfect for keeping that right leg from wobbling."

"I'd be happy to, Howard," I said.

"Try not to forget," Howard said. "For me, it's an important book."

New Well Blues

August 17, 1986

IN THE YARD of the old house we go to in the summer, we have just had a new well dug. When we had the old well, water restrictions sometimes had to be imposed by what our family calls the Water Committee. I have always been the chairman of the Water Committee. That meant that I always had to do the dishes, since I was afraid that anyone else might use too much water. Now all of that is over. The new well is a grand success. I should be a happy man. The well-digger is a happy man, or will be when I pay him.

"Why do I find myself missing the old well?" I asked my wife the other day.

"I hope it's not because we won't need a Water Committee anymore," she said. "You've taken your chairmanship so seriously lately that the girls and I were beginning to think you might start listing it on your résumé."

I couldn't imagine where my wife got the idea that I was overserious about my responsibilities as Water Committee chairman, unless she misunderstood the sayings I used to quote to myself to keep my spirits up while I scrubbed the pots and pans ("Command is a lonely task").

"As it happens, I will be stepping down as chairman of the Water Committee imminently," I said, in an appropriately dignified tone. "As soon as I finish the final draft of my resignation letter."

"I'm sure you don't regret not having to talk about the well all summer," my wife said.

I suppose not. Still, we did have some nice talks about the well. One of the things I like about well discussions is that everyone has a different theory about the principles governing wells. A well discussion is one of those it-all-has-to-do-with discussions — people saying it all has to do with the water table or it all has to do with aquifers or it all has to do with cones of depression. Talking about wells is like talking about how fireplace flues work or about why dogs are particularly apt to bark at mailmen.

On the theory that an effective Water Committee chairman must educate his people in the principles of intelligent conservation, I worked out what I considered a clear, scientifically sound presentation on how wells work. At least once a summer, I would give the presentation to my daughters, illustrating the movement of the underground water table with a perforated straw in a drinking glass. The day I realized they were old enough to understand the presentation was the day one of them said, "Daddy, I think that's the most boring thing I've heard in my whole life." In that sense, the old well was a boon to discipline. For years my wife merely had to say, "Clean up your room or I'll ask Daddy to explain how wells work."

"You're not thinking of the Parkers, are you?" my wife said.

The Parkers are the only other summer family in our area — a husband and wife who are both terribly involved in their jobs all year and always savored August as the only time they could spend quietly with each other. They had the same sort of old well we had, and we often joined them in long, circular discussions about how to get more water — whether digging deeper would provide a larger reservoir or block the existing spring, whether it was true that a drilled well didn't produce water of real quality. Then one summer they drilled a new well. It was a grand success. Their water problems were over. The next summer, things started to go wrong between the Parkers.

In the absence of discussions about the well, Joe Parker noticed that his wife didn't have an awful lot to say. Mary Parker found that Joe's army stories didn't really wear terribly well after the first fifty or sixty tellings. The Parkers broke up. These days their house is occupied by a shifty-looking fellow who uses the front room to rent out adult videos.

I wasn't thinking about the Parkers. My wife and I still find plenty of things to talk about. Just last week, for instance, we had an interesting discussion about how fireplace flues work. Once I was reminded of the Parkers, though, I said, "I didn't much like the taste of the water from that drilled well of theirs" — hoping, maybe, to spend a few minutes on drilled wells, just for old times' sake.

Just then, one of my daughters came into the room and said, "There isn't any water." Our water pump had burned out, ruined beyond repair.

A knowledgeable neighbor told me we would need a

new one — a half-horsepower pump maybe, although a one-third-horsepower might do just as well. "The question," I reported to my wife, "is how far it has to lift the water if you count the depth of the well but then you factor in the distance to the house plus the slight rise of the yard."

"That's an interesting question," she said.

"Yes, and I haven't even mentioned the advantages and disadvantages of a piston pump versus what's called a jet pump," I said.

"Maybe we should talk it over," she said.

Secrets of the Deep

August 24, 1986

SOONER OR LATER all this publicity about underwater exploration is bound to renew interest in launching an expedition to find out once and for all what animal Surf 'n' Turf comes from. It's been a full three years since my breakthrough hypothesis. Working solely from the evidence of what's presented to someone who orders Surf 'n' Turf in an American restaurant — a slab of red meat and a shellfish claw — I deduced that a surfnturf might be a tiny aquatic Hereford. I envision it as a shell-covered beast that moves through the depths slowly, in herds, and can moo and draw flies under water.

It's only a hypothesis. I am not one of those researchers who become wedded to their own theories and ignore even the most compelling evidence if it tends to support some opposing view. If surfnturfs turn out to be huge creatures that look more like beefy crawfish, fine. I won't say I'd want to raise them, but I would certainly accept scientific proof of their existence. Also, I'm not one of those researchers who assume that their projects have to be first in line for research funds. If the Navy and the Woods Hole Oceanographic Institute think that poking around the staterooms of the *Titanic* is more important than searching out a marine creature basic to American cuisine, fine. I'm certainly not going to be the one to say that serious researchers consider these meanderings through the First-Class Lounge to be on the order of a television stunt. If others want to say such things, fine.

Now that the point has been made by others, I might just add that I blame this entire show-biz approach to underwater exploration on Jacques Cousteau. I know you're not supposed to blame anything on Jacques Cousteau. He's the only unassailable Frenchman besides Marcel Marceau. Since I loathe mime, I happen to think Marcel Marceau also has a lot to answer for. When the French government refused to allow our bombers to cross French airspace on their way to bomb Libya, I thought I knew of a perfect way for our government to indicate its displeasure — assuming, of course, that the folks in the White House did not choose to indicate their displeasure by taking out, say, Avignon with a couple of ground-to-grounds. We could have revoked Marcel Marceau's visa.

But at least Marceau is not responsible for holding up scientific research. In fact, he may have inspired the subjects used in an important study gauging the correlation between people who insist on not talking while on stage and people who have nothing to say. It's Cousteau I blame for diverting much-needed funds from the hunt for the elusive surfnturf at a time when we had the momentum to track the beast to its underwater lair (or pasture).

Cousteau's programs had something in common with

national political conventions: the point was to pretend it wasn't all being done for television. "Ze divere, Jean Pierre, weel poke ze shark on ze nose," Cousteau would say as Jean Pierre was lowered off the boat. "Ze purpose of zis is to study how much ze shark likes being poked on ze nose."

Now Cousteau is honored at the White House and the Navy is photographing teacups on the *Titanic* and fortune hunters are taking millions of dollars in treasure off sunken ships in Florida and serious underwater research on the surfnturf is languishing — leaving the field to those airheads who think the surfnturf is a land-based mammal, maybe some sort of crablike moose.

As it happens, I'm not one of these purists who think that we researchers can't use the resources of modern communications. I can even envision a Cousteau show on the search for the elusive surfnturf. Jean Pierre, fleeing from an enraged shark, comes across a patch of ocean floor that looks strangely like a prairie. He hears mooing. He sees flies. He spots some tiny creatures with brown and white markings on their shells. They are grazing. They are swatting at the flies with their claws. The surfnturf has been discovered. I am proved right, once and for all. The moose crowd eats crow, served with lobster claws.

Fear of Chiggers

August 31, 1986

YOU MAY BE UNDER the impression that this terrible case of poison ivy I've got has at least caused me to worry less about mosquitoes. Wrong.

It's true that several times a day I say, "This feels like sixty thousand mosquito bites." But that doesn't mean that I no longer dread mosquito bites. If you're asked by the dentist what your sore tooth feels like when he blows a jet of air on it, the fact that you say "It feels like you just stabbed me with a red-hot poker" does not mean you would like him to rummage around in those little drawers dentists have, find the old poker he knew he kept around someplace, get it red-hot, and then stab you with it. I know because I recently had this very conversation with our dentist, a man I'll call Sweeney Todd. I managed to stop him just as he was heating up the poker.

My wife thinks I have an unnatural fear of mosquitoes. Wrong. If she had my fear of mosquitoes it would be unnatural, because mosquitoes don't bite her. I'm quite aware that if she had poison ivy she wouldn't go around saying "This feels like sixty thousand mosquito bites," and people would think she was being brave. But it wouldn't be a matter of bravery: she doesn't know what sixty thousand mosquito bites feel like. I do.

It's a scientific fact that some people are more likely than other people to be bitten by mosquitoes. I am the most likely of all. My attraction for mosquitoes is so great that people who have some reason to walk near stagnant ponds or swampy marshes sometimes ask me along as a means of drawing off attackers, the way a quarterback who intends to pass might first send a decoy halfback into the line without the ball in the hope of having him jumped on by the opposition's largest and most vicious linemen.

During the summer months, I could probably make a living hiring myself out as a sort of mosquito lightning rod for company picnics and family outings and Sunday afternoon double-headers. I could list myself in the Yellow Pages under MOSQUITOES, DIVERTER. It's not a career I aspire to, of course. Being a mosquito diverter at a Sunday double-header between a couple of pennant contenders could mean getting, say, sixty thousand mosquito bites — or the equivalent of a case of poison ivy. I've already got a case of poison ivy.

I've tried to be brave about my case of poison ivy. I say "This feels like sixty thousand mosquito bites" only four or five times a day. No more than half a dozen other times daily I may say something like, "Oh woe is me!" or "This must be pretty much what Job went through." That's brave. If I weren't being brave, I'd say, "This feels like four or five chigger bites." I'm thousands of times more afraid of chiggers than I am of mosquitoes, even though

I got my last chigger bite when I was a boy in Kansas City many years ago. It still itches a little.

My dictionary describes a chigger as "a 6-legged mite larva (family Trombidiidae) that sucks the blood of vertebrates and causes intense irritation." Intense irritation! Whoever wrote that has never been the vertebrate whose blood was being sucked. Also, the writer doesn't even mention how many chiggers can hide in a tiny patch of tall grass or how each chigger bite has an itch-power equivalent to approximately fifteen thousand mosquito bites. He obviously was brought up in the East, a chigger-free region that also happens to value understatement; he probably defines sharkbite as something that can cause "considerable discomfort."

It isn't easy to explain chiggers to someone who grew up in the East — someone like my wife, for instance. I've tried. I've tried to explain the duration of a chigger bite's itch: "Just short of eternal." I've tried to describe what sort of protective clothing or insect repellent is useful against chiggers: "None." I've tried to describe the remedies that can stop a chigger bite from itching: "Amputation, sometimes."

If you grew up in the Midwest, part of the way you look at any part of the world from then on has to do with chiggers. A couple of years ago, a high school friend of mine named Joe Don asked me how I could stand living in New York, which he visited for three days in 1964 during a meeting of Motorola dealers who had nearly met their quota. "It's crowded and it's noisy and there's no place to park and if you just pick up your foot to walk down the street they'll steal your shoe," Joe Don said.

"Joe Don," I said, "there are no chiggers in New York."

Joe Don looked stunned. He stared at me for a minute. Finally he said, "Not even in the high grass?"

"There isn't any high grass," I said. "They took away the high grass, just in case."

There's plenty of high grass where we live in the summer, but there aren't any chiggers. Where we live is many hundreds of miles northeast of where the most northeasterly chigger bites have ever been reported. I avoid the high grass anyway, just in case. In fact, it was when I was backing away from some a couple of weeks ago that I found myself in a patch of poison ivy.

The Inside on
Insider Trading

September 7, 1986

"DADDY, WHAT's insider trading?"

"Isn't it customary in most families for the daughter to come down to breakfast and ask the father if she can buy some sweater that is essential to her continued existence?"

"Definitely."

"Then why are you asking about insider trading instead of whether you can buy a new sweater?"

"Can I buy a new sweater?"

"Certainly not."

"That's why."

"What kind of cereal do you want this morning? How about a bowl of this stuff that fulfills your basic daily requirements of Niacin, Lipides, and Riboflavin until March of 1994? That would be a real load off your mind — not having to worry about Niacin, Lipides, and Riboflavin all that time. It would leave you free to worry about whether your breakfast is rich enough in Thiacin and Pantothenate."

"That kind of cereal is gross, Daddy."

"Now that I think of it, Niacin, Lipides, and Riboflavin sound like some lawyers I used to know. If you think the cereal is gross, you ought to meet Lipides."

"Daddy, you know what Mommy always says: she says if you never give me a straight answer I'm going to grow up to be a smart-aleck like you."

"I thought 'Certainly not' was a pretty straight answer to the sweater question."

"Daddy, what's insider trading?"

"O.K. Insider trading is when someone who works on Wall Street gets information that is not available to the general public and uses that information to make money buying or selling stocks. It's like opening your eyes in hide-and-seek before you've counted to a hundred."

"What happens to someone who gets caught at insider trading?"

"He gets arrested."

"But what's his punishment?"

"His punishment is that he has to tell on someone else who's doing the same thing."

"Don't they ever have to go to jail?"

"Well, maybe if —"

"I know, Daddy: maybe if they're represented by Niacin, Lipides, and Riboflavin."

"May I recommend a bowl of this stuff that gives you the same amount of energy the Olympic decathlon champion gets every morning at breakfast? Then if you're only interested in maybe a little shot-putting you'll have a lot of energy left over."

"What I don't understand, Daddy, is what people who work on Wall Street do who aren't doing something you can get arrested for."

"They try to get information that is not available to the general public and then they use that information to make money buying and selling stock."

"You mean none of them keep their eyes closed while they count to a hundred?"

"Right. Some of them get their eyes kind of squinty, but even those peek through the slits between their fingers. There was one guy on Wall Street years ago who kept his eyes closed until he counted as far as twenty-five or thirty, but he went broke."

"But if everyone who works on Wall Street does the same thing, why are just some of the people on Wall Street arrested?"

"Those people are arrested for stealing too fast."

"I don't think Mommy would call that a straight answer, Daddy."

"Well, it's a lot like the speed limit on driving. It may be true that everyone drives faster than fifty-five, but that doesn't mean that you can whiz past a state trooper who's doing sixty and not expect to be pulled over to the side. It's the same with those people in the New York Parking Violations Bureau who got indicted for taking bribes from contractors. If they had just waited until they left government and then taken cushy jobs with the contractors, nobody would have said anything. They got indicted for exceeding the speed limit. That's really what people are accusing Michael Deaver of — speeding."

"What docs Michael Deaver have to do with it?"

"The federal law on conflict of interest says that after

you leave the government you have to wait a certain amount of time. Then you can start getting rich by, say, collecting favors from the people you helped get into the government yourself. If you don't wait the certain amount of time, you might get stopped for speeding. Deaver says that the last time he looked he was going maybe fifty-eight or sixty; some other people say that two different troopers had him clocked at a hundred and five."

"Is that your straightest answer — that business about exceeding the speed limit?"

"Why do you think people are always talking about the risks of life in the fast lane?"

"Could I please have a bowl of that cereal that's chock full of Riboflavin?"

"Sure. Anything else?"

"Yes. I think I need a new sweater."

"No problem."

Tax Reform Blues

September 14, 1986

MY FRIEND HOWARD, who often worries, told me that the man who prepares his tax returns called the other day to say that there was some rather embarrassing news to report.

"I can imagine your response to that," I said to Howard. "Something like 'Do you think they'll give me time to pack and say good-bye to my family?'"

"Well, not exactly," Howard said, with what I can only describe as a thin smile. If I hadn't known Howard for years as a particularly solid citizen, I might have been concerned for a moment that I had stumbled on an embarrassing little felony.

"Let me guess what the embarrassing news was," I said. "The folks in Washington love the F-111 fighter-bomber your tax man's clients chipped in to buy for them last April 15th, but it turns out that they already have too many F-111 fighter-bombers, so they'd like you to contribute just a little more so they can return the fighter-bomber and, by adding the extra money to that, get themselves a new post office in Spokane."

"That's a very good guess," Howard said, rather formally. "But that's not it. It had to do with the new tax reform law."

"Don't tell me," I said. "The prospect of tax reform has so depressed your accountant, who was sensitive to begin with, that he is abandoning his practice, and he's embarrassed to have to ask you for a few bucks to tide him over while he's having himself retrained as a metallurgist."

"No, that's not it," Howard said, and for the first time I realized that he looked particularly glum.

"So what was the embarrassing news?" I asked.

"He had run the last-year returns of all his clients through the computer to see how they'd do under the new tax reform law," Howard said, "and it turned out that I'd pay less."

After Howard said that, he paused and stared out in space for a while. Since we were carrying on this conversation in Brewster's Drug Store, where we had run into each other one Saturday morning, he was actually staring out at a display of skin lotions. The effect was the same; he looked truly miserable. I waited for him to continue, but after a couple of minutes I realized that he was finished.

"Wait a minute, Howard," I said. "Did I miss something? Where's the embarrassing part?"

"With tax reform, I'd pay less," Howard repeated, and he looked as if he might cry, right there in front of a rack full of shampoo and hair oil and what Brewster's labels "Grooming Aids."

"But that's great, Howard," I said. "Maybe you can take Edna to Hawaii. I don't understand why you find this so sad."

"Haven't you read all of the articles about how people are going to be affected by tax reform?" Howard said. "They say that the people who may have to pay more taxes are the ones who had figured out how to work all these tax angles the new law's going to eliminate — people who had been buying things that somehow depreciate a hundred percent without disappearing, people who were writing off their back yard as a money-losing cattle ranch. I'm going to pay less. That means I've been paying through the nose all these years. Everyone's going to think I'm a dope. The IRS might as well just send me a sign to hang around my neck: SUCKER."

"But there's no way for anyone to know about this," I said. "In fact, I'd be willing to spread the word that you're going to lose a fortune under the new law because you'll have to quit writing off your Plymouth as a shrimp boat and you can no longer claim to be an unpaid employee of a foundation run by your six-year-old daughter."

"Thanks, but it's too late," Howard said. "Edna already told half the people we know. She thought it was good news, poor thing."

"I'm sure she didn't realize what she was doing," I said.

"Oh, I'm not angry at her," Howard said. "In fact, I feel terrible about not providing her with the tax shelters some of the other guys have given their wives."

"C'mon, Howard, you've always been a good provider," I said.

But Howard seemed intent on running himself down. "No, this whole thing has made me realize that I haven't really been responsible enough financially," he said. "This year, with both of the older kids in college, I've even had to get into a lot of debt."

I tried to think of something to cheer Howard up. "Isn't the interest on that deductible?" I finally said.

"I guess," Howard said. "I haven't got around to talking with my accountant about it."

"Wait a minute," I said. I went around to Brewster's magazine rack, grabbed one of the news-magazines, and turned to the piece on tax reform. "Listen to this," I said to Howard. "Personal debt interest is deductible, but it isn't going to be deductible after the tax reform bill gets phased in. You're going to lose a big tax dodge. I guess you pay plenty of interest."

"Oh yeah," Howard said, beginning to brighten. "I owe a bundle."

"You've been done in by tax reform," I said. "Those brutes have torn down your shelter."

"Hey, you're right!" he said. "Whadaya know about that! Wait till I tell Edna!"

"Congratulations," I said. But he was already out the door of Brewster's and half running down the street toward home, a happy man.

Geography Lesson

September 21, 1986

I'VE DONE EVERYTHING to avoid facing up to the geography crisis. It's not that I haven't seen the evidence. Every week I seem to read about the results of yet another study confirming a shocking level of geographical ninnyism among the young. Apparently, if you asked the average American high school student where, say, Alabama is, he might identify it as the capital of Chicago, which he thinks of as a large country somewhere in the Middle East. A high school student who lives in Montgomery or Birmingham or Huntsville wouldn't say that about Alabama, of course; he'd say it was a football team.

I tried to ignore all of this. When I'd hear what percentage of American college sophomores identified London as a small country in France, I'd say something like, "Well, kids'll be kids." After all, every week I was also reading about the results of studies demonstrating ninnyism in any number of other fields. In the United States there is a firmly established custom of sending researchers around the country to prove to ourselves how dumb we are. The newspapers are constantly running results of surveys showing what percentage of citizens don't know who their congressman is and how many of them, when presented with a multiple-choice question, identify *haute cuisine* as the French foreign minister. I myself live in fear that one day, as I'm walking innocently down the street, I'll be accosted by some smart-aleck survey-taker who will demand that I give him the name of the secretary of labor.

For a while, I tried to persuade myself that students don't mean these answers to be taken literally. That sort of thing happens sometimes with geography. Once, just after I had spent a few days in Baton Rouge witnessing what seemed to me particularly bizarre behavior in the Louisiana legislature, a man I knew in New Orleans tried to put it all in perspective for me by saying, "What you have to remember about Baton Rouge is that it's not the southern United States; it's northern Costa Rica." He didn't mean it literally, I figured, so why assume that college freshmen are being literal if they happen to identify Baton Rouge as a continent very near Cambodia?

But I realized that I was just kidding myself. I realized that I wasn't facing up to the geographic crisis because I resented the fact that American students no longer seem to value what happens to have been my best subject. I didn't do very well in math — I could never seem to persuade the teacher that I hadn't meant my answers literally — but I was a whiz in geography. Even now I remember that Lake Titicaca in Peru is the highest deepest lake in the world (other lakes are higher and other lakes are deeper, but no lake is both higher and deeper). Even now I can name the leading mineral products of Missouri (lead and zinc). Who were these wise-guy students to act as if such knowledge was not worth having!

That's when it hit me: students do tend to be wise guys. Maybe what's portrayed as a geography crisis is actually an elaborate prank played by high school students on whichever institution is spending a lot of grant money trying to gauge the depth of their abysmal ignorance. I can imagine more or less the same scene being repeated all across the country. Three or four high school boys are lounging around a local video-game parlor when they are approached by a carefully dressed man who is carrying a clipboard. He asks them if they would volunteer to answer a few questions for a survey, in return for which the next round of Pac-Man will be on him.

"Ronnie Joe here can help you," the boys say, pushing forward a slack-jawed young man whose haircut suggests an Apache who is toying with the idea of going over to the Rastafarians. As it happens, Ronnie Joe is the captain of the high school geography team — a geography ace who has, in state competition, rattled off the capitals of Burkina Faso and Luxembourg, correctly answered a question about which mountain ranges are found in Hungary, and recited the principal products of Surinam in the order of their importance.

"Where is Russia?" the researcher asks.

"Two down from Bolivia," Ronnie Joe says, looking proud.

"What is the Danube?"

"A punk waltz group," Ronnie Joe says as the researcher solemnly scratches away at his clipboards and Ronnie Joe's friends try to conceal their giggling by hiding behind the video games.

The researcher gets what he came for and is promoted to the survey that shows how dumb grownups are. A week later he stops me on the street and asks me to name the secretary of labor. I tell him that I can't seem to remember the name right off hand. He makes a notation on his clipboard, thanks me, and walks away — not realizing that I'm in on the joke.

Corporate Triumphs

September 28, 1986

I WOULDN'T WANT it thought that I have no big-time business ambitions at all. Occasionally I muse a bit about how much I might like being fired from a high position in a major American corporation. My latest inspiration is Thomas Wyman, who recently got booted out as chief executive officer of CBS. Never again will Thomas Wyman enter a room full of strangers with the certain knowledge that at least one of them is bound to grab him by the lapel and ask him why CBS sit-coms are so imbecilic; for that emancipation, he picks up somewhere between two and five million dollars, depending on how the severance agreement in his contract is interpreted. The more I read about Wyman's firing the more I realize that, even at two million, it's my sort of thing.

I suppose those grim young business-school strivers I'm always reading about still nurture a vision of corporate success based on the high-powered executive in the Hollywood movie who strides out of his office toward the board room, tossing off orders about reports and conferences and telephone calls as he goes. They see themselves as the chief executive officer of, say, JKL Industries, a holding company that holds mostly holding companies. When I see that high-powered executive in a movie, all I can think about is having to sit through all those meetings and return all those phone calls and read all those reports. In my occasional daydreams of corporate success, I see myself about to leave the board room, having just been fired as chief executive officer of JKL Industries. I'm standing at the door, my hand on the knob, as the chairman of the board says, "Frankly, you've run this company like the South Vietnamese Army."

Around the long, mahogany table that's used for board meetings, the other directors nod in assent. One of them says quite loudly, "Glad to see the back of him." I hear another mumble something that sounds like, "What a turkey!" I try to look solemn, or even chagrined. The chairman says, "You can pick up your four-million-dollar severance package from Miss Pritchard in accounting."

I do. Reaching for the check, I realize that I will no longer have to hold all of those holding companies that are, in turn, holding companies, some of which are themselves holding companies. I will no longer, in other words, feel like a Christmas shopper loaded down with too many packages. I can simply open my arms and let everything I'm holding fall to the ground. For that I get four million dollars. I know for certain now that this is my sort of thing.

I would have thought that by now even those strivers who claim to like sitting through meetings and returning telephone calls and reading reports might share my notion of what constitutes business success. It's been clear for

years, after all, that in the world of huge corporations
there's nothing more lucrative than being fired well. In
its 1986 annual issue on executive compensation, *Business Week* reported that if it had included income from
severance agreements in its charts, five of the ten
highest-paid corporate executives would have been people
paid for leaving rather than for working. The highest-paid
executive on the chart got $12,739,000 for a year's work,
which sounds like a nice piece of change until you hear
that Michel C. Bergerac, who had been chairman of
Revlon, got thirty-two million dollars for hitting the
bricks.

Of course, not everyone can aspire to learn enough
about lip gloss to become the chief executive officer of
a cosmetics company, but the CBS power struggle was a
reminder that these days you don't even have to be a
CEO in order to stop at Miss Pritchard's desk. Van Gordon
Sauter, the head of CBS News, was shoved out the door
with Wyman, and the papers said he would get about two
million dollars. Sauter's best-known mistake as an executive was to turn the *CBS Morning News* over to Phyllis
George, the former Miss America, who was widely ridi-
culed as a bubblehead and finally driven off the air. These
days, Phyllis George gets a million or two a year from
Miss Pritchard, she sleeps as late as she wants to, and
nobody calls her a bubblehead. No wonder.

The new chief executive officer of CBS is Laurence
Tisch, who owns a quarter of its stock. He is now the one
who gets to listen to the constant complaints of the local
station managers. It will be up to him to pacify ego-
maniacal television stars. It is now Tisch who enters any
room full of strangers with the certain knowledge that

at least one of them is bound to grab him by the lapel and ask him why CBS sit-coms are so imbecilic. Also, since he is rich enough to consider just about any check from Miss Pritchard the equivalent of tip money, he can't even look forward to a lucrative firing. Somehow, he is referred to regularly in the newspapers' coverage of the power struggle as the winner.

Using It All

October 5, 1986

LAST WEEK, my friend Howard, who often sees the dark side, appeared to be particularly deep in the dumps. In that state, Howard resembles a basset hound who has just been told the bad news about the results of the worms test. When I asked him what the trouble was, he said something that sounded like, "I've never even made a mackerel."

"Howard, only God can make a mackerel," I said. I figured that might cheer him up a bit. So many people get dejected because of unrealistic expectations.

"Not mackerel," Howard said. "Macro."

It turned out that he was talking about a way to rig up a word processor so that some phrase you use all the time is typed out every time you hit a single key. From what Howard told me, a copywriter who specializes in television ads can fix one key to type "This offer void where prohibited" and another one to type "Use only as directed" and another to type "Younger-looking hair."

I reminded Howard that he was not an advertising

copywriter, that he used his word processor mainly for writing weekly letters to his mother in Fort Wayne, and that it somehow seemed inappropriate to use the full capacity of modern circuitry to create a way for a single key to produce "Well, Mom, not much new to report this week."

"But that's just it," Howard said. "I'm using this magnificent machine just to write my mom in Fort Wayne. Do you realize that my computer is capable of producing a spread sheet?"

"I think I might find that more impressive if I thought either of us knew for sure what a spread sheet was, Howard," I said. I was tempted to leave it at that. Howard is virtually impossible to shake out of the doldrums if he's wearing his wormy-basset-hound look. Also, I remembered what happened a few years ago when he became dejected because he felt he wasn't truly taking advantage of his pocket calculator.

"I've never used the pi function," Howard said to me at the time.

"Howard," I said. "You only use your calculator to keep track of your checking account. Why would you need the pi function?" As I said that, I must admit, it occurred to me that since no more conventional method had ever enabled me to reconcile my checkbook with my bank statement, I might see what happened if I crumpled my bank statement into a ball and then calculated the ratio of its circumference to its diameter.

"But that's just it," Howard said. "I only use my calculator to keep track of my checking account. I'm not using it to its full capacity."

As it happens, I can't imagine anyone being anything

but ecstatic about not using the pi function. As far as I'm concerned, a high school diploma is a coded message that actually says, "The Bearer of This Document Will Never Again Have to Worry about Pi." On Thanksgiving, when a lot of Americans give thanks for the American freedom that means the most to them — freedom to comparison-shop, maybe — I give thanks for a life free of pi anxiety. Except for that one day a year, my only consideration of pi since high school graduation came when the Texas legislature passed a resolution declaring pi to be an even three instead of 3.141592+. A lot of people made fun of the Texas legislature for that. Not me. To me it made perfect sense.

As I told all that to Howard, he looked sadder and sadder, as if he had been informed that in addition to the worms treatment he was about due for a distemper shot. It turned out that my mention of Thanksgiving had reminded him that his food processor was all but lying fallow, never having been used to make the special red-white-and-blue national holiday Jell-O mold that, according to the instruction booklet, was the work of a moment, thanks to the power and versatility of the deluxe model.

Despite my memories of that failed attempt to cheer Howard, I tried telling him that the macro function is probably used mainly by people who prefer hitting a single-key code because every time they type out the phrase it represents they feel guilty about the fact that it doesn't happen to be true — people like the Kremlin speechwriter who punches one key for "Nothing but anti-Soviet slander" or the White House briefer who has a key for "The President is being kept informed."

Howard responded to that with a look I can only asso-

ciate with a basset whose owner, faced with the incon-
venience and expense of protracted worming treatment,
has finally allowed himself to utter the words "Maybe
it would be better to put him to sleep."

I did the only thing I could think of. I knew Howard's
letter to his mother this week was going to concern how
guilty he feels about using his new ice cream machine
only for simple sherbets even though the instructions
say that it is capable of making a frozen marshmallow
daiquiri popsicle with the flick of a switch. Before he
wrote it, I had a computer-freak friend of ours hook up
Howard's machine with one macro. Now, whenever Howard hits the asterisk the computer types, "It pains me not
to be able to use the machine to its full capacity."

Deity Overload

October 12, 1986

I'VE BEEN READING all the commentary on the presidential candidacy of the Reverend Pat Robertson, hoping to find that someone has mentioned Deity Overload.

Self-serving? Sure. I'll admit that. I invented the term "Deity Overload" several years ago, and I'd obviously like to see it find its way into the language of American politics, along with "backlash" and "yuppie" and "big Mo" and "Super Tuesday" and "It's not over until the fat lady sings."

I might as well admit that despite my long-time devotion to the art of motto-making, I've never coined a phrase that has found its way into the language of American politics, although I think I came pretty close with "Never Been Indicted."

So it was natural that Robertson's candidacy — and his certainty it was part of God's plan for his life — got my hopes up. I could imagine one of those news-analysis pieces in the *New York Times* headlined CAPITAL GRIPPED BY SINGLE SUBJECT: DEITY OVERLOAD. I could imagine one of the Washington columnists with a particular inter-

est in language — William Safire, maybe, or James Kil-
patrick — tracing the origin of the term to a column I
wrote in 1983. I could imagine myself acknowledging
authorship with a modest little statement in which I also
manage to introduce some other promising phrases I've
been polishing as Robertson begins jockeying for the
Republican nomination with rivals like Jack Kemp and
George Bush — phrases like "the wacko right" and "the
wimp factor."

As a guest on one of the network commentary shows
some Sunday morning, I would say that the term "Deity
Overload" was coined early in the Reagan years, when it
became apparent that people like James Watt and Jerry
Falwell were seeking divine guidance for the sort of
political decisions that a boss of the Chicago machine
might assign to one of his ward captains. I would explain
that Deity Overload is a concept that does not challenge
the idea of an all-powerful God or an all-knowing God
but does raise the question of whether God is all-patient.

As I imagined those scenes of triumph, I also noticed
that nobody seemed to be mentioning Deity Overload. I
realize that Robertson's candidacy brings up a lot of other
theological issues to write about. After Robertson said
that running for president was part of God's plan for his
life, for instance, it was obviously tempting to speculate
about how to explain people who think God's plan for
their lives requires them to snooker Pat Robertson out
of the Iowa delegation. We would have to conclude that
either Robertson or the gang of delegate-grabbers got
God's plan wrong, but it might be difficult to find out
which one. If God filed these plans down at the court-
house, after all, we wouldn't need so many religions.

I can understand commentators taking up such questions before wrestling with the difficult concept of Deity Overload. I can understand that there are those who might want to speculate on how far down the hierarchy of political campaigns God gets involved. It may seem perfectly reasonable, for instance, that the Lord takes an interest in who is going to be leader of one of His most powerful nations — particularly considering the fact that the other most powerful nation is controlled by what is often called "Godless Communism," and may therefore be beyond His help — but what about, say, the current campaign for the governorship of Kansas? It may be that somewhere in the United States some candidate who has prayed mightily for his own election and has assured his followers of divine support is about to find in his mailbox a neatly typed but unsigned card that says "God does not do City Council races."

It occurred to me that some commentator who took that approach might find it natural to proceed from there to a discussion of Deity Overload. So far, nobody has. I suppose that's why I'm mentioning it myself. I've begun to face the fact that the term isn't catching on. I haven't given up, though. Like a lot of the candidates, I'm waiting for a miracle at the convention.

The way I see it, the elements that were present when I invented the term in 1983 are still present. Ayatollah Khomeini is still haranguing God constantly. The Israelis are still waving copies of an Old Testament contract promising them Judea and Samaria. Some Roman Catholic bishops are still maintaining that the Lord desires the defeat of candidates who do not support the church's position on abortion. There is the usual amount of war, pestilence, plague, and starvation for God to deal with. If Pat Robertson looked heavenward from the Republican convention and asked whether the divine plan for his life could be adjusted to accommodate a deal to trade his delegates for a say in the vice-presidential nomination, isn't it possible that God might finally say "Enough's enough"? That would be Deity Overload.

Touched by the
Little Touches

October 19, 1986

A LOT OF PEOPLE assume I'm the sort of person who hasn't spent much time in hotels fancy enough to concentrate on "the little touches." If you came over to my house, I could show you a pile of fancy soap and miniature shampoo bottles that say otherwise. I've been around — which is why the incident with my shoes came as such a shock.

I know those little-touches hotels. They have a terrycloth robe in each room. They deliver the morning paper. They sometimes furnish complimentary limousine service around downtown, implying that they consider you the sort of person who could show up for his appointments in a limousine without causing people to point and giggle. They furnish real clothes hangers with hooks on them, implying that they may even consider you the sort of person who doesn't steal hangers.

As a little European touch, a little-touches hotel will even have your shoes shined if you leave them outside the door at night. It's the only little touch I'd never taken advantage of — although I suppose you could argue that I didn't really use the limousine service that time in Houston when I asked to be driven to a 7-Eleven to get some shaving cream and the concierge told me the limousine was busy. My reluctance to leave my shoes was based on a story I once heard: apparently, during an official diplomatic visit to Washington some years ago, the Prime Minister of Finland left his shoes outside his door at Blair House and woke up the next morning to find that they had been donated to the Salvation Army.

Last week, though, when I checked into a little-touches hotel in the Southwest, the bellhop seemed particularly keen on having me leave my shoes outside the door. I inspected him closely, trying to decide if he looked like someone who might head a gang of shoe thieves that snatched old brogans, spirited them off to a garage in a dilapidated part of town, stripped them of their laces and tongues, and sent the shells to South America disguised as 1978 Ford station wagons.

He didn't look the part. Also, I had decided to trust the hotel. After all, they trusted me with their hangers. Also, the terrycloth robe they had provided me — a terrycloth robe that had a hood on it, as a little touch on the little touch — had not even come with the usual notice warning me, in a backhanded and subtle kind of way, that I'd be billed and maybe even arrested if I decided to steal it. I left my shoes outside the door — even though, unlike the Prime Minister of Finland, I don't travel with an extra pair.

Early the next morning, before stepping into the shower, I opened the door a crack to get my shoes. There was nothing outside my door except the morning paper. I closed the door. Maybe it was too early. After I had taken a shower and slipped on my terrycloth robe, I opened the door again. There were shoes outside the door. They were somebody else's shoes.

Not only that: they were somebody else's gigantic shoes. They were not simply long. They were wide. They were high. A playful cocker spaniel could have hidden in either one of them. I tried to think of where I had seen such shoes before. I remembered attending a circus side show as a child. I was standing in front of a giant, who leaned slightly to one side, like a tree that had grown too big for its roots. I was saying to my friend Eddie, who stood next to me, "Will you get a load of his shoes!"

I tried phoning the concierge, hoping that he wouldn't have any way of knowing that I was the guy who got turned down for the 7-Eleven run in Houston. The line was busy. I decided that I could simply find my own shoes outside another door and make the exchange. I walked down the hall with the giant's shoes in my hand, still wearing my terrycloth robe with the hood. It occurred to me that if another guest passed me in the hall he might take me for some kind of deranged and excommunicated monk on his way to conduct a shoe ritual.

It also occurred to me that if the giant spotted me I might be hard put to explain what I was doing with his shoes. He was certain to be out of sorts, having spent the night with his feet hanging three or four feet over the end of the bed. As I crept along the hall, struggling with the huge shoes, I expected any moment to hear a booming voice from behind and above me. I wondered if he would start by saying, "Fee, fi, fo, fum . . ."

I turned one corner of the hall and then another, and then I spotted my shoes. Gently I lowered the giant's shoes to the floor. Then I snatched up my shoes, raced down the hall, ran into my room, and slammed the door. I thought I heard rumbling in the hall outside, but it might have been my imagination. I was safe. I had my shoes. With a feeling of great relief, I looked down at them. They were not shined. I called up the concierge and asked to be driven to a shoeshine stand. He said the limousine was busy.

Columbus Sailed
the River Blue

October 26, 1986

I WAS DELIGHTED when the National Geographic Society announced, after a five-year study, that Christopher Columbus's first landing in the New World was almost certainly on a tiny Bahamian island called Samana Cay. I thought my Uncle Harry might finally abandon his theory that the *Nina*, the *Pinta*, and the *Santa Maria* first touched land at Kansas City, near the corner of Eleventh and Walnut.

What gave me hope is that Uncle Harry, in attacking rival theories to the Kansas City landing, has always pointed out that scholars who believe Columbus first landed in the Bahamas have never been able to agree on precisely where. "The islanders don't even know which island," he always says, "and I've got the exact intersection." Uncle Harry has always referred to people who believe in the Bahamian landing as "the islanders" — a habit that led me as a child to envision scholars like the late Samuel Eliot Morison of Harvard singing calypso or diving for conch shells.

Even as I read the impressive array of evidence gathered by the National Geographic Society's researchers, though, I reminded myself that my Uncle Harry is not a man who gives up a theory easily. In the words of his wife, my Aunt Rosie, "Harry's about as flexible as a tree stump."

As far as I know, Uncle Harry still holds unwaveringly to every theory I heard him express while I was growing up in Kansas City. For instance, he still believes that no matter how many calories are involved, you can't gain any more weight than the weight of the food you've eaten. Anytime my Aunt Rosie warns him about the inevitable results of his consuming, say, an entire pound of double-dipped chocolate cream candy, Uncle Harry says, "So I'll gain a pound. Big deal!" If Aunt Rosie asks how he knows that you can gain only a pound from eating a pound of chocolate, she invariably encounters his final, uncrossable line of defense on any subject: "It stands to reason."

During the first part of my childhood, I found it easy enough to go along with Uncle Harry's theory about the discovery of America. After all, I had found him an ally on any number of other issues. He was a firm believer, for instance, in the theory that consuming ice cream fairly early in the day "gets the corpuscles moving," and he insisted that early bedtime was the leading cause of slow-wittedness in children.

Whenever I was in a car that drove by the corner of Eleventh and Walnut, a busy intersection in downtown Kansas City, I would say, "This is where Columbus landed." I don't know how to explain the fact that nobody ever contradicted me. Maybe it's an example of how far

Midwesterners will go to avoid confrontation. Maybe the public schools of Kansas City didn't truly buckle down when it came to teaching about the voyages of Columbus. Maybe Uncle Harry didn't stand alone after all.

There came a time, of course, when I was forced to confront Uncle Harry with the fact that Kansas City was at least nine hundred miles from the nearest ocean.

"I guess you never heard of rivers," he said. Harry's theory was that Columbus went right past the Bahamian islands ("Hitting one of those little bitty islands from Spain would have been like throwing a strike from deep center field"), crossed the Gulf of Mexico, sailed up the Mississippi as far as what is now St. Louis, took a sharp left at the Missouri River, and went across the state of Missouri to land at Eleventh and Walnut.

When I'd point out that the theory required believing that Columbus sailed against the current for hundreds of miles on two different rivers, Uncle Harry would always say, "If he was the sort of man who took the easy way, he'd have stayed in Spain and danced the flamenco." When I'd point out that Eleventh and Walnut is a good mile from the Missouri River, he'd always say, "Big deal!"

After I moved away from home, I'd send Uncle Harry any article I ran across on unconventional theories about the discovery of America — say, some amateur scholar in upper Minnesota claiming that, centuries before Columbus, Leif Ericson had made it to the outskirts of St. Cloud. I suppose I was hoping that such theories would make Uncle Harry see how bizarre his own notions on Columbus's voyage looked to an outsider. He would agree that whoever entertained the idea of Viking ships crossing the Minnesota plains had lost touch with reality, all right, but he'd take that as a confirmation of his theory that living too long in a place that stays cold into April can "freeze up thirty percent of the usable brain cells."

Still, it was with some optimism that I phoned Uncle Harry to discuss the National Geographic Society announcement with him.

"I was hoping you'd see that," he said. "It shows that the islanders are desperate to counter the specificity of the Kansas City landing. Mark my words: they'll study another five years and then they'll come up with an intersection."

"Do you mean that this makes you even more certain that Columbus landed at Eleventh and Walnut?" I asked.

"Of course," Uncle Harry said. "It stands to reason."

The Gipper Lives

November 2, 1986

MOST PEOPLE DON'T KNOW that the real George Gipp — the George Gipp of "win one for the Gipper" fame, the George Gipp played by Ronald Reagan in *Knute Rockne, All American* — is still alive. That's right.

Yes, I realize that in the movie George Gipp died, so that Coach Knute Rockne could invoke the name of the Gipper in the great half-time pep talk that inspired Notre Dame to go out there and wipe up the field with what had been up to then a pretty rugged Rensselaer Polytechnic Institute eleven. But not everything they say in movies is true. That's right. In real life, as it happens, George Gipp survived. In real life — now that we're being absolutely factual about all of this — Notre Dame lost the game. RPI creamed them. In real life, as a matter of fact, George Gipp only went to Notre Dame because he couldn't get into Holy Cross. That happens to be the truth.

How do I know? Because George Gipp told me. I visit him pretty regularly. He lives in an old-age home in Massapequa, Long Island, these days, and keeps himself in pretty good shape stiff-arming nurses' aides and dying bravely off camera. His memory is absolutely phenomenal, and he's in good spirits, particularly considering the fact that he's had to go through most of his life being assumed dead. As you might imagine, just about every person he has ever been introduced to says something like, "But I thought you were — well . . . uh . . . Nice to meet you, Mr. Gipp." Apparently, though, he learned to deal with that a long time ago. He usually just says to the person, rather quietly, "Stick it in your ear, buddy."

He's been particularly cheerful this fall, ever since he started monitoring Ronald Reagan's campaigning for Republican senatorial and congressional candidates. Every night, when the network news comes on, George Gipp and some of his friends can be found in the nursing home's television lounge, sitting in front of the twenty-six-incher. He's armed with two or three Magic Markers and a large map that shows the congressional districts of the United States. I happened to be in the lounge several weeks ago on the evening that a clip of Reagan campaigning for a senatorial candidate in Louisiana showed him saying to a cheering crowd something like, "So this November I want you to win one for Louisiana, win one for your country, and, if I may add a personal note, win one for the Gipper."

Mr. Gipp and the other people in the lounge started cheering, and a couple of old gentlemen came up to clap Mr. Gipp on the back. Mr. Gipp, smiling broadly, got out one of the Magic Markers and ceremoniously colored in the entire state of Louisiana. By his count, that made twenty-eight states or congressional districts in which Ronald Reagan had asked the voters to win one for the Gipper.

I hated to spoil Mr. Gipp's fun, but I felt I had to ask him if it struck him that the President was being just a tad insincere by saying "Win one for the Gipper" in twenty-eight different election campaigns.

"Oh no," he said. "Rockne — the real Rockne — did the same thing. You know, I was pretty sick when he made the original speech — don't let anyone tell you that anything hurts worse than an impacted molar — but I played every game the next year, and every single half-time Rockne said, 'Win one for the Gipper.' He said it with me sitting right there in the locker room. After a while, some of the players started saying, 'Coach, wasn't the Swarthmore game last week the one you told us we were supposed to win for the Gipper?' Sometimes Rockne would say he couldn't remember ever saying that, and sometimes he would remind us that we had lost the Swarthmore game, not to speak of the Kenyon game and the MIT game, so, in fact, we hadn't really won one for the Gipper yet and it was about time we did."

"Excuse me, Mr. Gipp," I said, "but I didn't realize Notre Dame lost to schools like Swarthmore in those days. I've always seen the Notre Dame team of that era referred to as a football powerhouse."

Mr. Gipp smiled. "That was the spin Rockne put on it," he said. "Swarthmore murdered us. But Rockne was careful never to admit that, except to us in the locker room. After the game, he always told the sportswriters how proud he was of the Fighting Irish. By the next September, he'd be saying that it'd be hard to repeat an undefeated season that had seen us whip teams like Michigan and Ohio State and Army. The sportswriters never seemed to point out that we hadn't played those teams and that the teams we had played, like Haverford and Oberlin, had slaughtered us. He was a charming man, Coach Rockne."

"Oberlin!" I said. "Notre Dame was slaughtered by Oberlin!"

But Mr. Gipp, lost in his recollections, seemed not to hear me. "When I read in the paper that Reagan left the summit in Iceland cussing about his failure and two days later decided it was a big triumph, it really brought back those memories of Coach Rockne," he said. "That's exactly how the Coach would have handled it. Yes sir, the President learned all that at Notre Dame."

"But the President didn't really go to Notre Dame," I said. "That was just a movie. You're the one who went to Notre Dame."

"Only because I couldn't get into Holy Cross," he said.

My Life in Art

November 9, 1986

SOMEHOW IT GOT OUT that my turndown record in submitting cartoon ideas to *The New Yorker* is a hundred percent. This is very embarrassing to me, since a lot of my high school friends back in Kansas City have always assumed that most cartoons in *The New Yorker* are based on my ideas. In fact, some of my high school friends are under the impression that I'm responsible for a number of cartoons each month in *Playboy* — only the tasteful ones, of course — and that other cartoon-carrying magazines like *Collier's* and the *Saturday Evening Post* would have survived if they had just been able to hold out until I got to New York and hit my stride.

The truth is that my turndown record at *Playboy* is also a hundred percent and that some historians of American magazines believe I hastened the death of *Collier's* and the *Saturday Evening Post* by bombarding them from Kansas City with bad cartoon ideas. This is all very embarrassing. I suppose it had to come out sometime, but I wish it could have come out about somebody else.

For years, I took some pride in never allowing myself to get discouraged. When I first started submitting cartoon ideas to *The New Yorker* in 1963, I tried to find something encouraging in the phrases used by the art department editors in their notes of rejection — phrases like "This is the dumbest idea I've ever seen" and "I can't imagine what makes you think this is even remotely funny" and "Are you some kind of nut case?"

There came a time when the language of the notes left little room for an encouraging interpretation ("If you do not cease harassing this office with cartoon ideas at once, we will be forced to hand the matter over to our attorneys"). Even then, I did not give up. By chance, I had just thought of one of my most brilliant cartoons. A fat woman dressed in riding clothes is patting a horse on the nose and holding out her hand in the way people do when offering a horse a lump of sugar, except that she's holding a bottle of saccharin pills. Funny, huh? I decided to circumvent the oppressive art department bureaucracy by going directly to a cartoonist.

Maybe this part of the story will at least serve as a lesson to some of the young people in Kansas City who have literary aspirations. They tend to think that the key to getting published is to get to New York and meet the right people. Wrong. I knew these cartoonists — we had offices on the same floor — and it didn't do me any good.

"Why is the woman fat?" a cartoonist I'll call Melvin said. "Why isn't the horse fat?"

"Nobody likes a nit-picker," I said.

"It would be hard to draw the label on the saccharin bottle so people could read it," a cartoonist I'll call Clarence said.

"It wouldn't be hard for somebody who didn't have fat fingers," I said. I was getting a little testy. In fact, I might as well admit that the two cartoonists in question don't have names like Melvin and Clarence; I just gave them those names because I'm still mad at them for refusing to draw my cartoon.

I was not discouraged. I never allowed myself to get discouraged. I began approaching other cartoonists. By chance, I had just thought of another great cartoon. It's in a children's zoo where kids are encouraged to feed the rabbits. One kid is holding out some lettuce for a rabbit, and there's a long line of kids waiting their turn. The rabbit says to the kid, "Thanks awfully. It was delicious. But I couldn't eat another bite." Funny, huh?

Oddly enough, I found that some of the cartoonists were edging away from me in the lobby of the building. When I started telling them some of my cartoon ideas in the elevator, they would get off at the second or third floor, even though their offices were on the eighteenth floor and both the second and the third floors were completely occupied by the home offices of an orthopedic shoe manufacturer. After eight or ten years of that, I began to allow myself to get discouraged.

For the next ten years or so, I didn't offer cartoonists any cartoon ideas. They started talking to me again at the water fountain. When the revelation about my turndown record came out, in fact, I happened to be talking to Melvin — someone I finally started referring to a couple of years ago as Scott. He told me that the magazine had stopped buying cartoon ideas from noncartoonists years ago. I was sorry to hear it, of course. There's been a lot of turnover in the art department by now, and I sort of thought I might try recycling the one about the horse and the fat woman.

"That's a shame," I said. "I've always felt that my two true talents were cartoons and parallel parking."

"Hey," he said. "That's not a bad idea for a cartoon."

"You mean the horse and the fat woman?" I asked, wondering how he remembered after all those years.

"No," he said. "A guy standing at a cocktail party saying, 'My two true talents are cartoons and parallel parking.' Or maybe 'one-liners and parallel parking.' A guy with a sort of dopey look on his face."

"I did not submit that as a cartoon idea," I said. "It has not been officially submitted. Dopey look!" But Melvin had already pulled out his pen and was moving toward his office.

Confessions of a Crank

November 16, 1986

THE QUESTION ABOUT those aromatic advertisements that perfume companies are having stitched into magazines these days is this: under the freedoms guaranteed by the First Amendment, is smelling up the place a constitutionally protected form of expression?

This is a complicated issue. For instance, let's say that the manufacturers of a chic new perfume called Slap ("When a woman wants to say 'Go ahead and hit me' ") produce a magazine advertisement that looks pretty much the way all magazine ads for perfume look these days: that is, it shows an attractive young woman with a torn blouse being knocked against the wall by an unshaven lout whose agent has been telling him for years that in a certain light he has a striking resemblance to Richard Gere. The manufacturers decide that infusing the ad with the actual smell of Slap would be preferable to attempting a description of it — particularly since the three most poetic phrases mentioned by randomly selected people asked to describe its aroma were "eagle in flight," "new-mown cabbage," and "low-tide breeze."

Let's say that the manufacturers have a constitutionally protected right to smell up the magazine page they have bought and paid for. Fine. But how about the author of the article on the facing page, which now smells strongly of Slap? He has worked for months on a piece extolling the caramelized pastries found in the remote Popolizio region of southern Italy. Now his pastry descriptions are going to be read by people who are at the same time getting a whiff of cabbage. What about *his* rights?

Let's consider a subscriber to the magazine, a teenager who has always claimed that she is allergic to cabbage. Let's consider the subscriber's father, who, opening an envelope that has spent the day in the mailbox next to the aromatic magazine, discovers that a reminder from the Diners Club about last month's unpaid bill is even more dispiriting if that reminder smells faintly like a large feathered beast. Do these people have rights that are involved here? They may, but those rights seem to be in conflict with Voltaire's famous comment to Helvetius: "I may not like the way someone smells but I'll defend to my death his right to smell that way!"

Some people may be surprised that I see so many sides to the aromatic advertising issue. They expect me to dismiss aromatic advertising in two or three simple and exceedingly nasty sentences. Why? Because they think I'm a crank. I'm aware of the reputation I've been getting for crankiness. It's all right. I don't mind being thought of as a crank. In my heart of hearts, after all, I know that I am a sympathetic and genuinely sweet-tempered person. What I do mind are people who expect all cranks to rail against certain features of American life that have become designated crank targets — features of American life like aromatic perfume advertisements and tear-out subscription cards in magazines and canned music that plays on the telephone when you've been put on hold.

"I guess I know how you feel about canned music that plays on the telephone when you've been put on hold," one of these people will say to me once he has been assured that my crank papers are in order.

No, he doesn't. Here's how I feel about it: it's a complicated issue. Let's consider the position of people who believe that a piece of music is something that has to be listened to rather than something that can be used as aural wallpaper. When they're finally put through to the purchasing agent they've been trying to reach for weeks, they might have to say, "Could you please put me back on hold? There are another twelve or fourteen bars to go in the Montavani." But let us also consider the person who spends every second that he's on hold thinking that he might have been cut off — because of some slight congenital displacement of the eardrum, he has never been able to distinguish between the complete silence of hold and the complete silence of having been cut off — and is grateful for any sound that indicates otherwise. This is not a simple issue.

I suppose I'd be decertified as a crank if I admitted that I do not have a simple loathing for tear-out subscription cards. In fact, I use them sometimes. Not for subscriptions. I use them to send little messages to the people who work in what magazines call the circulation fulfillment department. I think it's nice to buck people up now and then — that's not an unusual thought for a sympathetic and genuinely sweet tempered person — and in this case it doesn't even cost me a postage stamp to do so. The subscription cards always have prepaid postage on them. Sometimes I just send along a simple word of encouragement ("Keep up the good work, circulation fulfillment people") or share an aphorism ("If you can't say something nice, don't say anything at all, creep"). Sometimes I chat about what's in the magazine. Occasionally, I even mention aromatic perfume advertisements — in which case I always say, right at the start, "It's a complicated issue."

The Gipper Still Lives

November 23, 1986

NOW IT TURNS OUT that some people didn't believe me when I reported that I had found George Gipp — the George Gipp about whom Coach Knute Rockne said "Win one for the Gipper," the George Gipp played by Ronald Reagan in the movie — in an old-age home in Sandusky, Ohio.

They don't believe that in real life George Gipp, who died so nobly on the screen, survived his illness (an impacted molar), or that he only went to Notre Dame because he couldn't get into Holy Cross. They don't believe that in real life the Notre Dame football team lost the game it had been asked to win for the Gipper — lost it to an aroused Rensselaer Polytechnic Institute squad, which had been exhorted at half-time to "win one for the principle of logarithmic function." They don't believe that Notre Dame actually lost most of its games in those days, to schools like RPI and Swarthmore and MIT. They think I made all of those things up. I'm not so much angry as a little bit hurt.

Some people wrote to say that Knute Rockne could not have been the one who taught Ronald Reagan how to turn defeats into victories — you call them victories, and if someone points out that they were actually defeats, you change the subject — because Reagan didn't go to Notre Dame in real life, even though he keeps referring to himself as the Gipper. They said that there is definitely a distinction between real life and the movies, despite the fact that the President once mentioned as an example of inspiring patriotism a heroic act that turned out to have been from a World War II bomber movie starring Dana Andrews.

I didn't relish the prospect of facing Mr. Gipp with the news that a number of people considered him unbelievable. If you had spent most of your life meeting people who were under the impression that you had died in the second reel, after all, it couldn't be much fun learning that you might have been invented by somebody who's not even inventing at screenwriter rates. I could picture him there in Sandusky, peacefully gazing out on the rolling Vermont hills, trying to remember whether he was the one with the ranch in Santa Barbara, and wondering for the thousandth time whether a D in Latin from the saintly and vicious Sister Mary Magdalene was what kept him out of Holy Cross.

But I knew it was my responsibility to tell all of this to Mr. Gipp face to face, particularly if I actually had made him up. That seems truly unlikely, of course — although I haven't been completely confident about the line between fiction and reality ever since it turned out that the story the President keeps telling about the welfare mother who picks up her check in a Cadillac is something he remembered, in a slightly muddled form, from a movie in which the character played by Rhonda Fleming used a Lincoln to pick up her maid (played by Akim Tamiroff).

So it was with some trepidation that I crossed the lawn of the Seaview Harbor Rest Home, under a hot Arizona sun, and asked for George Gipp — the Gipper. He was sitting in the TV lounge, where I had visited him during the recent election campaign.

"There seems to be some question about your existence, Mr. Gipp," I said. I think it's always better to get these things right out on the table.

Mr. Gipp seemed not to hear me. He was studying what he called his "Gipper map" — the map he had used to keep track of how many different electorates President Reagan had asked to win one for the Gipper. When he looked up he said, "It was just like having Rockne back again."

"But the President played *you* in the movie, Mr. Gipp," I said, reminding him that Knute Rockne was played by the late Pat O'Brien, now ambassador to Belgium.

"Reagan learned all this postgame spin-talk from Rockne," Mr. Gipp said, tapping the map. "We lost every game that Rockne told us to win for the Gipper, too — the Swarthmore game, the Oberlin game. But you wouldn't have known it to hear Rockne talk."

"I wish the people who don't believe in your existence could hear you say that, Mr. Gipp," I said.

"Look at what Reagan said about the election results that showed his senatorial candidates getting creamed all over the country," Mr. Gipp told me. "He said the results 'brought pretty good news.' He said he's pleased he was able to get across the message of how important it is to have a firm defense. Those are almost the exact words

Rockne used after Swarthmore beat the bejeebers out of us."

"Then it doesn't bother you that just about all the races he asked people to win for the Gipper were lost?" I asked. "After all, you're the Gipper."

Mr. Gipp smiled, thinking back on the old days. "It was Rockne all over," he said. "It usually took Rockne about six months to start talking about the undefeated season we'd had. I figure by spring Reagan will have managed to interpret the fact that the Republicans won the governor's race in Arkansas as a national mandate for Star Wars."

"I'm glad you're taking all this so well, Mr. Gipp," I said, not wanting to upset him with the news that the Republicans had lost the governor's race in Arkansas.

"It almost makes me wish I hadn't croaked in the second reel," he said.

I left him there, lost in his memories, and walked out into the cold Wisconsin rain.

Missouri Uncompromised

November 30, 1986

I CAN'T IMAGINE why these political commentators keep saying that the recent senatorial elections failed to put any major issues before the American people. In Missouri, the choice presented to the voters on how to pronounce the name of the state could hardly have been more clear-cut. There may have been some collateral issues — I understand someone said something about all the farmers going bust — but I don't think the Missouri results can be interpreted as anything but a referendum on the pronunciation question. I don't care what you might have heard from the White House about how the President has taken that election as a clear mandate to do under-the-table arms deals with creeps.

Not major? Is that what I heard somebody say — not a major issue? How, may I ask, can you decide policy for a state you can't even pronounce? What would you think if Margaret Thatcher pronounced Great Britain as if it were spelled Great Bribben? Imagine her looking hard into the television camera, with that visage that reminds you of

the expression your junior high school principal wore just
after that mysterious flood in the faculty lounge, and
saying sternly, "Malingerers and layabouts must be told in
no uncertain terms that they will be given no quarter in
Great Bribben."

I don't mean to give the impression that the pronunciation of Great Britain was a big issue in this year's
senatorial race. Traditionally, foreign policy doesn't carry
much weight in Missouri campaigns. The issue was how
to say Missouri. As it happens, Missouri is my home state,
although I've been visiting in the East for the past twenty-
five or thirty years. In the interest of full disclosure, I
should also say that I made my own position clear on this
issue several years ago with a closely reasoned column
proving that Missouri is properly pronounced as of it were
spelled Missour-ah, and that those who take on Eastern
airs by pronouncing it as if it were spelled Missour-ee
should be shown floor-wax commercials until they recant.
In other words, if you're looking for an objective analyst of
the campaign results, I'm ideal.

I'm proud to say that the politicians in my home state
do not straddle the fence on this one. Yes, I've heard there
was once a wishy-washy gubernatorial candidate who tried
to play both sides of the street by saying Missour-eh, or
maybe Missour-oo, but he was soundly defeated and forced
to move to Arkansas in disgrace. This fall, the candidates
for the Senate seat being vacated by Thomas Eagleton
gave the voters a clear choice. Christopher Bond, the
former governor, pronounces the name of the state correctly. His opponent, Harriett Woods, who probably has a
lot of nice qualities of her own, does not.

Christopher Bond won. The campaign was clearly

fought on pronunciation, and no matter what the White House says, the President's impact on that issue had to be minimal, since he gave the impression at a Bond for Senate rally in Kansas City that he believed himself to be in South Dakota (which he pronounced correctly).

I have to admit that the election of a Missouri senator who said Missour-ee would have presented a rather awkward situation for me, since one of my standard responses to Easterners who consider my pronunciation quaint is that every single Missouri senator agrees with me — Senator Danforth and Senator Eagleton both having been first-rate on this issue over the years. My other standard response is "Buzz off, Easterner."

I can assure you, though, that this personal interest had nothing to do with my phoning a Missouri political analyst I'll call Joe and asking whether he interpreted the election as a repudiation of the Missour-ee faction by just plain Missourians.

"Either that or it shows that Republican sophisticates like Bond have figured out that Missour-ah sounds folksier for the voters," Joe said.

"Republican sophisticates!" I said. "Christopher Bond was born and raised right there in Mexico, Missouri."

"But he went to Princeton," Joe said. "Danforth went to Princeton too. Maybe it's a Princeton pronunciation."

"But how about Eagleton?" I countered. "Eagleton's a Democrat. Eagleton didn't go to Princeton."

"No, Eagleton went to Amherst," Joe said. "Maybe at Princeton and Amherst they say Missour-ah and at Williams and Dartmouth they say Missour-ee."

"But Joe," I said. "You say Missour-ah yourself."

"That's right," Joe said. "I thought it would make me fit

in better when I moved here from Brooklyn."

"Brooklyn!" I said. "From the way you talk, I always thought you were from Springfield, or maybe Joplin."

"These issues are never clear-cut," Joe said.

Unisys Revealed

December 7, 1986

TODAY'S REMINDER OF WHY Japanese industry is having our guys for breakfast is the announcement that the new computer company formed by the merger of Burroughs and Sperry will be called the Unisys Corporation. At a news conference, the chairman of Unisys, W. Michael Blumenthal, said the new name will signify that the two corporations are solidly one. Here's another interpretation: it will signify that the new corporation is run by people too dumb to think of a name.

I can imagine Blumenthal standing up there in front of the Unisys seal, explaining that, depending on what the board of directors decides about which syllable to accent, the new company either will emulate the perseverance Unisys demonstrated in his efforts to get back to Greece after the Trojan wars or will not require its employees to wear unisys clothing. Either way, he must have implied, it will do everything in its power to live up to what the public might expect of a company that sounds like a disease.

Blumenthal, of course, was the secretary of the treasury who was canned by Jimmy Carter. A Japanese executive in a similar situation might have committed hara-kiri, but Blumenthal decided instead to become chief executive officer of Burroughs at a salary of approximately nine hundred thousand dollars a year. If Blumenthal were asked to justify his decision not to take the honorable way out, I suppose he would argue that he got fired simply because Jimmy Carter was convinced by his pollster, Patrick Caddell, that dumping four or five Cabinet secretaries was one of two steps necessary if he wanted to revive his presidency, earn an enduring reputation for true statesmanship, and be swept into office for a second term.

The other step Caddell urged, you might remember, was for Carter to tell the American people that they were suffering from a national malaise — thereby guaranteeing that they would forget his accomplishments, fix him in their minds forever as a wimpy downer, and vote overwhelmingly for Ronald Reagan (who might have had trouble remembering his running mate's name but at least knew enough to tell the American people that they were the grandest little people ever). Oddly enough, Caddell didn't commit hara-kiri either. He's still greatly in demand as an adviser to politicians. In fact, considering the results of the Burroughs-Sperry name search, it occurred to me that Blumenthal might have let bygones be bygones and hired Caddell to come up with a new name.

That's not the way it happened. According to the article I read, a corporation-naming contest was held among employees of both Burroughs and Sperry, and 31,000 entries were received. Christian Lee Machen, a software systems manager in Atlanta, combined elements of the words "united" and "information" and "systems" to form Unisys. He won with that — which leads me to believe that of the 30,999 other contestants, 30,998 must have submitted the name Edsel and one suggested that the new company be called Not IBM.

This entire process was presided over by an "identity consultant company" called Anspach, Grossman, Portugal, Inc. Apparently, identity consultant companies are often hired these days by a corporation's CEO to change the corporation's name into something that will sound flashy enough on Wall Street to make the CEO's stock options worth something. Anyone who wants to impress Wall Street obviously has to get rid of any suggestion that the corporation is connected with the stodgy and outmoded process of actually producing goods rather than fiddling with balance sheets. Presumably, that's why corporate identity consultants changed American Brake Shoe to Abex, which sounds like a quadruped belonging to the antelope family ("Out of the bush burst a great hopping abex"), changed General Cigar Corporation to Culbro, which sounds like an enforcer ("We could call in Culbro, but he plays rough"), and changed International Harvester into Navistar, which sounds like the celestial navigation system for a space tractor. I suppose some corporate identity consultant was responsible for changing the United States Steel Corporation to USX — a name I can never hear without thinking that it should be followed by the motto "American Porn Movies since 1880."

All of this leaves one question unanswered in the saga of how two respectably named corporations like Burroughs and Sperry ended up being called something that sounds like a term that speakers of some grotesque parentbabble might use to inform their two-year-old that the new baby girl is at least not twins ("Johnny, I'm happy to say that mommy is going to come back from the hospital with a nice little unisys for you"). The question is, why was all of this done by a firm with a name like Anspach, Grossman, Portugal, Inc.?

The first problem is that Anspach, Grossman, Portugal, Inc. sounds like a company with at least two identifiable human beings involved in its operation — always a strong negative influence in the stock market. Also, what's that country doing in there? If these people know so much about names, how come they're not called AGP Systems Ltd. or Agrop? I suggest they clean up their own act before they start trying to find a cure for the scourge of rampant unisys. Blumenthal would probably loan them Christian Lee Machen — or, as Machen's fellow software systems managers must call him now, Chrisleemach, Inc.

Kashfleau's Problem

December 14, 1986

YOU WILL BE RELIEVED to hear that the Wall Street trader I know from college, Martin G. Kashfleau, remains at large. Actually, that's not a terribly nice way to put it. What I mean to say is that Kashfleau has not been indicted yet. That doesn't sound too good either. I'll try again. I would like to announce that Mr. Martin G. Kashfleau, the distinguished financier and ascending Manhattan social figure, has not been named in any investigation of Wall Street trading practices currently being carried out by the Securities and Exchange Commission or the United States Attorney's Office, but remains terrified that one of his friends will rat on him. There. That ought to do it.

I used to see Kashfleau around town a lot — he was one of those high-powered financiers who always asked you what you were into, in the hope he'd be able to say he just got out of that — but fear seems to have driven him indoors. I can't say I blame him for being worried about the possibility that one of his friends might decide to serve him up to the Federales. From the way Wall Street traders have been ratting on their pals to save their own skins lately, it's obvious that none of these fancy business schools require a course in foxhole behavior. For all Kashfleau knows, he may be on discount special in some squealer's pre-Christmas sale.

I regret to say that from the moment the insider-trading scandal became public some of our classmates began playing little jokes on Kashfleau — hiring men in dark suits to follow him for a few blocks, say, or leaving the names of bail bondsmen on his answering machine.

They reported that you could tell right away how scared Kashfleau was by what his answering machine said before the beep: "Martin G. Kashfleau is not available to speak to you, and knows nothing anyway. He would like to make it clear that he has never traded on information not available to the general public, and that every penny he has made in the market is a result of plain dumb luck."

When our classmates had gone through all the bail bondsmen in the Yellow Pages, they began leaving messages of encouragement on his machine — messages like "You've got nothing to worry about, Marty, as long as you're certain you've only dealt with gentlemen."

After a while, the pre-beep message Kashfleau had on his answering machine started changing daily. "Mr. Kashfleau would like to make it clear that what he told some friends about Acme Bolt & Tube last year was based on information gathered from a *People* magazine story he happened to have read in his dentist's waiting room," it would say, or "Mr. Kashfleau would like to make it clear that the legendary two-hundred-button telephone at his desk has been used strictly for calling around to make certain that the old gents who spend their days watching the ticker in the back of stockbrokers' offices in retirement communities have the same information he does."

One of the pre-beep messages — "Martin G. Kashfleau would like to make it clear that the purpose of the extra-long tape that follows the beep is not to provide time for detailed insider-trading tips but to permit his aged and infirm aunt, who lives in Fort Myers, Florida, to list all of her symptoms in one call" — made Kashfleau's tormentors realize that they had time to put a short playlet on his answering machine. They held auditions among our class-mates to see who got to play the SEC agent.

Johnny Murphy, who won that part, opens the playlet by telling a trader who has been caught red-handed that the government would be interested in obtaining some incriminating tapes on the activities of one Martin G. Kashfleau.

"Marty Kashfleau's my friend!" shouts the trader (some-what overplayed by Pudge Hackenberry, a frustrated actor who ended up in insurance sales). "He gave me my start."

"You could help restore public confidence in the market," the SEC man says.

"Get lost," the trader says. "Marty was the best man at my wedding. I'm the godfather of his children."

"You'd be doing your duty as a citizen."

"Marty put me up for the squash club," the trader says. "You could pull my fingernails out and I'd never rat on Marty Kashfleau."

"We might be able to arrange for things to go a bit easier for you," the SEC agent says.

There's a pause. Then the trader says. "I hope we can strap the tape recorder to my ankle instead of my back. I find with these double-vent suits, a tape recorder on the back makes such a bulge."

I don't know the effect the play had on Kashfleau's state of mind, but it apparently convinced him that defending himself over his answering machine was futile. I'm told that the message is always the same these days. The voice says, "Martin G. Kashfleau, the Wall Street trader, remains at large."

I Come Clean, Finally

December 8, 1986

I'VE BEEN LIVING a lie. There. I've said it. When the American people are told all the facts, I think they'll forgive me, but maybe not.

These are the facts: In September of 1981, I wrote a column that launched a campaign to change the national Thanksgiving dish from turkey to spaghetti carbonara. I defended my position vigorously. When traditionalists told me that we had to eat what legend says our ancestors might have eaten on the first Thanksgiving, I explained that one of the things I give thanks for every Thanksgiving is that those people were not my ancestors. In scholarly seminars about what really might have been eaten at that first meal, I described how the Indians, having had some experience with Pilgrim cuisine during the year, arrived with one dish of their own — that was the origin of the covered-dish supper in America — and that it was a dish their ancestors had learned from Christopher Columbus, whose Indian name was The Big Italian Fella. The dish was spaghetti carbonara.

In the frustrations of trying to get the movement off the ground during those early years, I might have been a bit intemperate in accusing the Turkey Lobby of terroristic tactics. Once or twice I might have mentioned the possibility that certain forces high in government had reason to make sure that the President would continue to be presented with a turkey every Thanksgiving instead of with a plate of spaghetti carbonara, whose appearance might remind voters too much of the White House table of organization chart. What we're talking about here is maybe a little overzealousness. We haven't come to the living-a-lie part yet.

Naturally, people wanted to know what my own family did for Thanksgiving. In 1981, I'm proud to say, my own family had a splendid Thanksgiving meal featuring spaghetti carbonara. Over dessert, I told our daughters the story of the first Thanksgiving — it ended with the Pilgrims calling spaghetti carbonara "the sort of thing foreigners eat" and the Indians calling the Pilgrims a bunch of turkeys — and my wife almost ruined everything by recalling childhood memories of her mother dishing out cranberry sauce and her father carving the Thanksgiving turkey and the cousins gathering in the parlor after dessert to hear her play recital pieces on the piano. For the next few years we were forced to eat turkey because we happened to be invited to other people's houses for Thanksgiving, but I stood by my principles: I berated every hostess for bending to the pressure of Turkey Lobby thugs. A leader has to lead.

We're getting to the part about living a lie. This year, for reasons I can't imagine, none of the people I had attacked for succumbing to Turkey Lobby scare tactics invited

us for Thanksgiving. My wife said she was pleased that
we would be having a family dinner at home — featuring
spaghetti carbonara. I was delighted. A local radio station
had offered to tape a Thanksgiving Day appeal for spaghetti carbonara — something I hoped to repeat annually,
like the Queen's Christmas message in England. I thought
I felt a ground-swell coming for our campaign. When I
went to Faicco's pork store on Bleecker Street to get the
pancetta for the spaghetti carbonara, the place was
packed. I immediately called in a tip to a local newspaper:
"I don't know if all those people were buying pancetta for
spaghetti carbonara, but I can tell you Faicco's doesn't
sell turkeys. This is beginning to look like a bandwagon."

Now we're getting to the George Shultz part. Like
George Shultz on the Iran arms sales, my wife began dis-
tancing herself from the policy. As Thanksgiving grew
closer, I heard her tell a few people about the traditional
Thanksgivings of her childhood. Once I heard her use the
word "depressing" in the same sentence with spaghetti
carbonara.

Then, on the afternoon before Thanksgiving, a friend
I'll call Rachel phoned. For complicated reasons, she had
decided at the last minute to have a traditional Thanksgiving, and she wondered if we'd be willing to drop our
spaghetti carbonara dinner and come to her house. A
turkey would be carved. There would be cranberry sauce.
One of Rachel's children, Max, would play his guitar for
the assembled and sing country-and-western songs —
including a new tear-jerker, composed by his first-grade
teacher, entitled "Too Many Long-Neck Bottles, Too Many
Red-Neck Men."

"Oh, please, let's do it," my wife said.

I looked at my daughters. "The Pilgrims were a bunch of turkeys," I said. "I taught you that."

"We want to hear Max play his guitar," my older daughter said.

On the way to Rachel's, I heard myself on the car radio assuring my fellow citizens that our family would sit down that afternoon to the traditional Thanksgiving meal of spaghetti carbonara. I turned to my wife. "I'm living a lie, Schultz," I said.

"Maybe if you tell the American people the whole truth, they'll forgive you," she said.

"I doubt it," my younger daughter said. "We learned in school that our ancestors put people in the stocks for lying."

"I've told you a hundred times," I said. "Those people were not our ancestors."

Conspiracy Maybe,
but No Plot

December 15, 1986

AFTER ONLY A WEEK or so of having the soap operas
pre-empted by congressional hearings on the Iran arms-
sale scandal, thousands of soap opera fans called the net-
works to demand their regular programs back. I wasn't
surprised. On *General Hospital*, nobody takes the Fifth.
Declining to answer a question may be perfectly support-
able on constitutional grounds, but it sure doesn't do
much for dramatic tension.

Occasionally someone on a soap opera may respond to
a question by saying something like, "I can't answer that
question now, Mark, but someday I will, and I hope that
when I do you and Brenda will realize that what I did I
did for you, whatever your father and the public health
authorities say." Usually, though, somebody on a soap
opera who is asked a question answers it, often at great
length ("Yes, Rob, I did realize that Bruce would someday learn of my combined face-lift and sex-change opera-

tion, but I thought I could buy time — time to heal the wounds Bruce suffered after Brenda's cat was eaten, time to pull my own life together so that what happened on the bridge that night between Hillary and Bruce's father and that perfectly dreadful Labrador retriever . . .").

In fact, television programming of all sorts is based on the assumption that anyone who is asked a question will answer it. If a tight end is asked by the sportscaster how it felt to grab that ball in the end zone with only thirty seconds left on the clock, he can be counted on to say, "It felt great, Tony." Even if he said "The next sportscaster who asks me how it felt to do something is going to find out how it feels to eat a football," that would be an answer of sorts.

If a contestant on a game show is asked if he wants to stop now that he has won $1,400 or try for the super deluxe toaster-oven that is valued at $3,200, he may hesitate for a moment to think it over ("Boy, a toaster-oven with power steering and factory air is just what I've always wanted . . . on the other hand, with $1,400 I could pay off the dog-track debt . . . on the other hand, if I quit now that knock-out blonde in the third row might think I'm a wimp . . ."), but he would never simply refuse to say.

If everybody got the idea that it was O.K. not to answer questions — if the dippy starlet on the talk show responded to a question about her love life by saying "None of your beeswax" — television could be crippled. Think of the letdown on a soap opera if Bruce Sutherland, the dashing but cash-short lawyer with the fatal auto accident and incestuous affair and severe acne in his past, asked Melissa Brent, the rich and extraordinarily attractive but

left-handed young widow, if she was indeed the one
with guilty knowledge of who ate Brenda's cat so that
Todd and Kimberly's divorce case had to go into extra
innings or if she'll marry him instead, and she said, "I
reluctantly inform you that, on the advice of my counsel,
I must decline to answer your question, based on the
rights afforded to me by the Fifth Amendment of the
Constitution." If that happened, the voice heard over
the theme music at the end of the show would have to say
something like, "Will Melissa marry Bruce? Is it possible
that Kimberly ate Brenda's cat? Tune in tomorrow, when
we will not find out the answer to any of those questions."

All of this must be why Republican senators and even
the White House people started calling for the witnesses
to quit taking the Fifth. Those Republicans don't want a
dog with a low rating on their hands. Oddly enough, I
think the hearings will do pretty well against the soaps as
soon the witnesses start talking. The lives of some of those
arms dealers the White House did business with sound
pretty much like what happened on the bridge that night
between Hillary and Bruce's father and that perfectly
dreadful Labrador retriever. A lot of the White House
people who say they didn't know about anything could
be taught to testify with the dramatic touch of a soap
opera character who acknowledges having been over-
whelmed by the complications in his past — the character who says, "Oh, sure, if I had noticed that my wife had
just left me and Joey had burned the house down and
my business had failed, sure, I might have acted differ-
ently toward you, Kimberly, but I was so preoccupied with
the question of who ate Brenda's cat . . ."

If the rest of the White House people decide not to answer questions, it would help, of course, if they did it more in the soap opera manner — something like, "I can't answer that question, but someday I will, and when I do I hope you'll realize that what I did I did for you."

Gurus' Shoes

December 22, 1986

THE BIG PROBLEM with being a guru, I've always thought, would be deciding what kind of shoes to wear. The rest of the guru outfit seems pretty straightforward. A saffron-colored robe is obviously the garment of choice. If you don't happen to have a saffron-colored robe, you could probably get away with wearing some other sort of robe and simply telling your followers that your robe is saffron-colored. After all, you're the guru.

Some aspects of the guru look don't even require the purchase of any special clothing. A beard is appropriate, for instance — a shaggy beard, to give the impression that your concerns are beyond such banalities as beard-trimming. Then you'd want what descriptions of gurus usually call "a beatific look" in your eyes. Actually, that's no cinch. I know because I practiced doing beatific looks in front of a mirror for almost an hour — disproving the ugly rumor that I don't do any research for these columns.

For a while, the best I could manage was a look that called to mind someone who, through some awful error at the veterinarian's, had just been given a shot that was meant for his pet Saint Bernard. Then I began imagining the voice of my mother saying, "If you don't quit making your eyes beatific they're going to stick that way." Finally I arrived at a look that seemed to be about as beatific as I was going to get.

"Would you call this look beatific?" I asked my wife.

"It's pretty much the look you have just before you nod off in front of the television set," she said.

I never quite got the hang of it, maybe because I've never been quite sure what "beatific" means, but I think it's safe to assume that someone who decides to go into the guru game has a pretty beatific look to begin with. Then he simply gets himself a saffron-colored robe. He grows a shaggy beard. So far so good. He's making a nice guru-like impression. But how about the shoes? Imagine the guru I've just described — saffron-colored robe, shaggy beard, beatific look in the eyes — and then imagine, peeking out from under the robe, a clunky pair of brown wingtips. There goes the ball game.

Shoes just don't go with robes. The Hare Krishnas who used to beat tambourines and chant on the busiest corner downtown suffered from that sartorial clash. Looking at one of them chanting away in his robe, you might think he was pretty otherworldly. Then you'd notice the high-top sneakers and realize that you were looking at some slightly squirrelly American high school kid snatched right out of the stamp club.

Sandals are not the solution they once were, although for a guru they've got cowboy boots beat by a mile. Those one-thong sandals that gurus used to favor as a symbol of pure simplicity are now manufactured by the millions as rubber "flip-flops" and used for walking back and forth to the shower at summer camp. A guru is bound to lose some respect if his followers glance down at his feet and wonder idly whether he left his soap dish and towel back in the tent.

What got me thinking of guru costume problems was a story I read in *Newsweek* about a woman named J. Z. Knight, who has apparently been raking it in as a guru in the Pacific Northwest. She's a new kind of guru. She says that in addition to her regular self she contains within her a 35,000-year-old male spirit named Ramtha. One of them has a blue Rolls Royce.

A woman who's hauling around a 35,000-year-old male spirit has a costume problem that goes way beyond anything that can be taken care of by a saffron-colored robe. Naturally, she's going to avoid clothing that's strongly identified with either one of her selves. If you're a woman who plans to have the voice of a 35,000-year-old male spirit come out of you during the service, you're obviously not going in there all got up in one of those ruffly ball gowns. And wearing what a male spirit wore for special occasions 35,000 years ago might be the sort of thing that could get you arrested.

Trying to dress somewhere in between wouldn't work: where would you go for 17,500-year-old unisex clothing? Apparently, J. Z. Knight decided instead to do what gurus call "fudging it a little." In the *Newsweek* picture, she was wearing a noncommittal costume that seemed vaguely familiar from one of the crowd scenes in *Gandhi*. Naturally, I looked down at her feet right away. She was barefoot. J. Z. Knight is one smart guru. Ramtha too.

My Senator

December 29, 1986

IMPORTANT PEOPLE always have a senator they can talk to in Washington. According to what was said in the last election campaign, for instance, when Wall Street moguls find themselves with a little problem on their hands, they call on Senator Alfonse D'Amato (R–N.Y.). If important people suddenly find they have need of a senator, they don't have to get out the Yellow Pages and start looking. I've been thinking that I ought to have a senator myself.

What if something comes up? What if the Veterans Administration loses my papers? What if the New York regional office of Social Security suddenly demands that I either submit any pre-1953 employment vouchers for summer jobs I held while I was growing up in Kansas City or face a fine or imprisonment or both? What if the United States Army Missile Command wants to plant an ICBM silo next to my house and the colonel in charge won't listen to my arguments that I'm enough of a target for the Russians as it is because of some remarks I passed about the quality of their cabbage soup?

"But you've never had any of these problems," my wife said when I told her about getting myself a senator. "Also, aren't those the kind of things you could talk to our own congressman about?"

I could if I could keep track of who our congressman is. The problem is that we live in Greenwich Village. Apparently, nobody wants to go to Washington as the representative of Greenwich Village, for fear the other representatives will take him for a hippie.

At some point, the powers in Albany seemed to start parceling out bits of our district to various congressmen, the way the sixth-grade teacher used to make each team take some of the kids who were so glonky they couldn't even handle right field. For a while we were represented by somebody from another borough who was identified so closely with the Koreagate scandal that the *Village Voice* got in the habit of following his name with the designation "D–Seoul." These days, I think we're represented by somebody from the suburbs of Syracuse, but he may have fobbed us off on the guy from Elmira in one of those back-room deals I'm always reading about.

Anyway, I don't want a congressman; I want a senator. With the possible exception of an Army second lieutenant, there is no impressively titled person anywhere with less influence than the average congressman. Also, it never occurred to me that my senator would be a New York senator. I'd be afraid that when I showed up at his office with whatever documentation I could come up with on the summer jobs in Kansas City, he'd leaf through the papers for a while and then say, "Kansas City? What are you — some kind of out-of-towner?"

That's why I thought for a long time about making Thomas Eagleton (D–Mo.) my senator. He's from my home state. Also, his staff once included a friend of mine, who left to go into the ice cream business — which means, in Washington terms, that I could be described as "close to Senator Eagleton."

But now Eagleton is giving up his seat. Of course, his successor, Christopher Bond, and I have both lived in Kansas City, although not at the same time. The other Missouri senator, John Danforth, is from the family that made Ralston Purina Dog Chow, which I used to feed regularly to my dog, Spike.

"It's not as if I don't have any connections left in the Missouri senatorial delegation," I said to my wife.

"I suppose your senator has to be from Missouri?" she said.

"Not at all," I said. "These years of living in the Village have made me much more cosmopolitan. I'm considering Nancy Kassebaum of Kansas."

Senator Kassebaum is from Topeka, which is just down the road from Kansas City. Also, her former husband went to my high school, although I didn't actually know him — which means, in Washington terms, that I could be described as "extremely close to Senator Kassebaum."

And I haven't ruled out Robert Dole (R–Kans.). It's perfectly possible that Senator Dole would find dealing with my Veterans Administration problems just the sort of thing that could put plenty of philosophical distance between him and George Bush (R–Teheran).

Once I select my senator, it will be easy to envision my visit to the office of the formerly intransigent Missile Command colonel. He's on the telephone — standing at full attention, looking nervous, and saying almost nothing but "Yes, sir" and "No, sir." When he hangs up, after agreeing profusely with the observation that there are plenty of other places in lower Manhattan to put an ICBM silo, he says to me, "It was your senator."

"Yes," I say, rather casually. "We're quite close."

Available for
Special Occasions

January 5, 1987

FOR SPECIAL OCCASIONS, you can now rent the following: a forty-foot limousine, the *Concorde* supersonic airliner, or the *Queen Elizabeth 2*. Never mind the price.

I just found out about the forty-foot limo and, in a way, I'm sorry to have to tell you about it. If you have a special occasion coming up, you probably thought you were only going to have to decide between the *Concorde* and the *QE2*. Now I've gone and complicated your life. Decisions, decisions.

On the other hand, I was certain that you'd want to know about absolutely every option. After all, this is a special occasion. Also, I've had trouble keeping news of the forty-foot limo to myself, because of the circumstances surrounding my discovery of it. You see, I actually spotted it, on Third Avenue, before I knew such a thing existed. The effect was as if a Japanese tourist — someone who had always assumed that the tallest person in the world was, say, five feet ten or eleven — arrived in America for his first visit, checked into the hotel, and walked onto an elevator whose other passengers consisted of the starting five of the Los Angeles Lakers.

For a while, my family didn't believe I had seen a limo that was, according to my estimate, almost precisely as long as our house. My wife thinks I'm prone to exaggeration. In fact, that's one of the complications in considering whether or not I should rent the *Queen Elizabeth* 2 for my wife's next birthday. Does it really make sense for me to rent an ocean liner for someone who thinks I'm prone to exaggeration and who may therefore believe, no matter how many of our friends are dancing the night away on the huge dance floor of the first-class lounge, that she's only on a PT boat? If you wife doesn't believe that you're prone to exaggeration, of course, you don't have that complication, and all you have to do is decide whether she might prefer the *Concorde*, or maybe a forty-foot limo.

What finally persuaded my family that the forty-foot limousine existed was that it was mentioned in a newspaper article. Its extras include three bars, the article said, but the story going around town that the drinks are served by a midget who can stand straight up inside the limo is untrue. I hadn't even heard the story, but I would have discounted it anyway: in my experience, almost all stories that include a midget are untrue. Also, no matter what you've heard, there is no hot tub in the forty-foot limo. (I find that most stories that include a hot tub are also untrue.) If you believed the midget bartender story or the hot tub story and you were basing your special-occasion plans on that, you may want to reconsider. Decisions, decisions.

I hate to complicate this further, but you should know

one disadvantage of renting out the *Queen Elizabeth 2*: From what I understand, a lot of your guests will be pre-occupied most of the time, trying to figure out how much it all costs. You'll be going around telling them to enjoy the floor show you flew in from Vegas and to take advantage of the aerobics class you've arranged out by the swimming pool, and they'll be costing out the fuel supply. Maybe your brother-in-law, who likes to appear jaded, will drop the subject after a comment or two ("We're talking about a couple hundred grand and change — no big deal"), but the rest of your guests will spend a lot of their time trying to find out what time-and-a-half would be for all those waiters. I agree that talking about the price of a special-occasion celebration is tacky. I know you didn't think your friends were like that. What can I say?

You wouldn't have that sort of problem on the *Concorde*, of course. There's no room for a floor show, and people don't really have the time to break out their pocket calculators and get into prolonged discussions about the price of the hors d'oeuvres. But those very facts can cause problems — people saying that a special occasion is so much nicer if someone like Tony Bennett sings, your Aunt Sophie griping that she brought her swimming suit for nothing, your brother-in-law complaining that flying faster than the speed of sound is no big deal if you're not going anywhere in particular.

If you're the sort of person who has trouble making up your mind, one solution might be to take people in the forty-foot limo to the airport, fly them to, say, London, on the *Concorde*, and then rent the *Queen Elizabeth 2* for the return trip. And bring your own midget. Or not. Decisions, decisions.

Wherefore Art Thou Nittany?

January 12, 1987

"DADDY, WHY IS the Penn State football team called the Nittany Lions? What's a nittany?"

"I thought girls were supposed to know all about football these days."

"Does that mean you aren't sure what a nittany is, Daddy?"

"Let me just give you the cereal choices for this morning: we have the kind with enough riboflavin to power the entire Southwestern Conference through the next three recruiting scandals and we have the kind that tends to get stuck in your teeth."

"That's all right, Daddy: I can just ask Mr. Hopkinson at school. He knows all about football. I'll have the kind with the riboflavin."

"Hopkinson's a blowhard. The man's got no historical perspective."

"You're not going to recite the starting line-up of the 1947 Kansas City Blues again, are you, Daddy?"

"I do know that it's lovely around Penn State in the autumn, undergraduates strolling hand in hand along the banks of the flowing Nittany."

"There isn't any Nittany River, Daddy. I looked it up in the atlas."

"It's ironic, of course, that Penn State is so famous for football, because classicists know it as the place where, some years ago, a group of brilliant undergraduate pranksters managed to fool half the scholars in the world with a bogus manuscript in ancient Greek that included a mythical mythical beast, the Nittany, and a scene in which Zeus asked Hera to return a token of his affection that seemed very much like a modern fraternity pin. I'll never forget the closing couplet: 'She nearly had a fit, and he / Rode off on a Nittany.'"

"No, Daddy. Not a mythical mythical beast."

"No?"

"Definitely not."

"Why can't you be interested in something like how the Georgetown Hoyas got their name?"

"Because Penn State's number one, Daddy."

"Well, you might take into consideration that a hundred years ago, when football began at Penn State, the area was known for its nittany mines. That semiprecious stone was in its heyday then. Sure, it later disappeared from jewelry stores almost overnight after the introduction of the artificial zircon, but at that time it was so important to the economy of the region that naming the Penn State football team in its honor seemed natural. But then the players complained to the coach. They said —"

"I know, Daddy: they said, 'We don't like being called the Penn State Semiprecious Stones, Coach.'"

"Right. Also, the cheerleaders complained that it just didn't sound right when they yelled, 'Go, go, Semiprecious Stones!' "

"Daddy, I think the kind with the riboflavin and the kind that tends to get stuck in your teeth are the same kind."

"In those early days of Penn State, of course, the mountain lion was quite prevalent in the region. People in Pennsylvania, being very orderly, categorized the various mountain lions according to which mountains they could usually be found in. The Pocono Mountains were actually the closest mountains to Penn State. But even then the Poconos were a resort area, so if the team had been called the Penn State Pocono Lions, people might expect them to come out on the field, do five minutes of stand-up comedy, and then announce that the special luau would be held by the pool at seven-thirty. So they compromised on Nittany Lions."

"Daddy, I think I'm going to be late for school."

"Of course, it could hardly be a coincidence that the first coach at Penn State, a hundred years ago, was the beloved Alonzo Nittan."

"Nittan, Daddy? That's a name?"

"That's right. Good Pennsylvania Dutch name, Nittan. The team was just called the Lions then. They had to play the University of Miami, which had a quarterback who could throw the bomb so well that he had been drafted by both the Union and the Confederacy."

"The forward pass came years later, Daddy. So did the University of Miami. And the Civil War was already over."

"Penn State was the underdog, and when they took the

field a cynical local sportswriter said, 'Those lions look a little kitteny.' To which a Penn State supporter is said to have replied, 'I think you'll find them rather Nittany.' And sure enough, they wiped up the field with the University of Miami."

"O.K., Daddy. I give up. How did the Georgetown Hoyas get their name?"

"I'd rather not say."

"I really have to get to school, Daddy. I'll let you know tonight what Mr. Hopkinson says about the Nittany Lions."

"On the other hand, I'm perfectly willing to reveal the line-up of the 1947 Kansas City Blues. They had Cliff Mapes in center field, of course. And in left, Hank Bauer, always referred to as 'rugged ex-Marine Hank Bauer.' And Eddie Stewart in right. Good old Eddie Stewart . . ."

The Old Stories
Are the Best Stories

January 19, 1987

I'VE FINALLY HAD to face the fact that President Reagan is no longer telling the story about the woman in California who picks up her welfare check in a Cadillac. I don't mean he's lost his sense of outrage at the luxuries this society bestows upon the destitute — he's got a new story about the New York welfare department putting up a homeless family in an expensive hotel — but for me, I now realize, things will never be the same.

For me, the story about the woman in her Cadillac had a comforting familiarity of the sort that flows from an oft-repeated story in childhood — like the story my Uncle Ed used to tell us about how, as a teenager in St. Joe, he was about to win a pie-eating contest when he had to leave because his mother called him home to supper. "Tell the pie-eating story, Uncle Ed," we always said when he came over. "Please tell the pie-eating story." I've always assumed that the President gets the same request when he goes to one of those black-tie dinners attended by true believers and rich nut cases: "Tell the Cadillac-lady story, Mr. President. We love the Cadillac-lady story."

What finally convinced me that he wasn't going to tell the Cadillac-lady story anymore was a *New York Times* account of a White House meeting at which Republican congressional leaders were invited to offer suggestions for the State of the Union message. "At one point, Robert H. Michel, the House Republican leader, urged the President to indicate his support of a Federal insurance plan to cover catastrophic illnesses," the *Times* reporter, Martin Tolchin, wrote. "Mr. Reagan responded by talking about a New York City welfare family living in a plush hotel at extravagant cost. Other leaders explained that catastrophic health insurance was not a welfare program, but Mr. Reagan reiterated his story about the welfare family."

The *Times* story reminded me that when it comes to talking about coddling the poor, the President's conversational style may be less reminiscent of my Uncle Ed than of my Uncle Harry, who still sometimes carries on about one of his pet theories in what those of us in the family call his "and furthermore" mode.

When Uncle Harry is particularly intense about, say, his theory that Columbus's first landing in the New World was in Kansas City, near what is now the corner of Eleventh and Walnut, he may answer some remark of mine like "It's nice to see Aunt Rosie looking so good" by saying "Columbus would obviously go due West, straight into the sun, once he took the left into the Missouri from the Mississippi."

Hoping I hadn't heard him correctly, I'd continue with something like "How's that trick gallbladder of hers holding up, Uncle Harry?"

"I read that one of those country music singers has a gallbladder-shaped swimming pool out behind his mansion," my Cousin Oscar would say.

"That's a new one on me," Cousin Thelma might say. "Spleen-shaped I've heard, of course, but gallbladder's a new one on me."

"And furthermore," Uncle Harry would say, "the accounts of the landing in Columbus's diaries fit Eleventh and Walnut to a T."

When President Reagan told the Cadillac-lady story — say, in answering a press conference question about whether he almost gave away the store by mistake when he met with Gorbachev in Reykjavik — it could conjure up any number of visions, depending on what kind of Cadillac you imagined. Sometimes I'd envision the Cadillac as a convertible, and the welfare recipient as a bejeweled bombshell who pulls into a No Parking zone, climbs out of her topless Coupe de Ville, and sashays into the welfare office, distributing vamp-like smiles to the regulars as she goes directly to the head of the line. Sometimes I saw a Cadillac limousine whose passenger, having decided not to send her driver in for the check because there might be some tiresome bureaucratic regulations against having one's welfare payments collected by one's chauffeur, steps regally from the car herself, saying, "I won't be a moment, Wentworth."

Now, I realize, all that is over. I don't mean to deny the impact of the new story. It conjures up a huge family of poor folks in a suite at what sounds like the Ritz — with the little kids trying to bean passers-by on the street below with boxes of designer soap and the teenagers ordering up crab legs from room service. I'm glad they're comfortable. But I worry about the Cadillac lady. I now see her as a worn-looking woman who arrives at the Los Angeles welfare office in a 1972 Cadillac that has an unpainted fender and a dragging muffler and a full load of hungry-looking children. When she finally reaches the counter, after a long wait in line, the clerk shakes his head.

"We don't have a check for you," he tells her. "Your story is no longer used."

The Cadillac lady seems devastated by the news, and the clerk tries his best to soften the blow. "All I can suggest is that you drive to New York," he says. "I heard the President say that the welfare department there puts poor people up at the Ritz."

I'll Take the Low Road

January 26, 1987

IF YOU THOUGHT I was above commenting on the *Washington Post* story that Secretary of State George Schultz may have a tattoo of a tiger on his backside, you overestimated me.

Of course, that's not the way I presented it to my wife when she said, as she watched me clip the story out of the *Post*, "You're not, are you?"

"A man must do what he must do," I said. "It's not always easy. Do you think it's fun to be the one who always makes the underhanded comment and passes the snide remark? When all the other columnists were talking about the legal and sociological questions raised by the Claus von Bulow trial, do you think I liked being the one who said that the only issue was whether he should get the chair for having added the 'von' to his name? Do you think I enjoy it when other children point to our kids in the playground and yell, 'Your daddy takes the low road — nah-nah, nah-nah-nah'?"

"Our kids have been too old for the playground for years," she said.

"Shhh!" I said. "There's no reason for the readers to know that."

The standard way to approach the issue of Shultz's tattoo, I figured, was to speculate on what other Cabinet secretaries might have tattooed on their backsides — presenting a column called "Tattoos of the Reagan Cabinet" in the way *Playboy* might present a photo spread called "Girls of the Savings-and-Loan Industry." I had already chosen a tattoo for Defense Secretary Caspar Weinberger — the Pentagon's new $30 billion B-1B bomber, artfully rendered to create the illusion that it is capable of flight — and I was starting to work my way down the Cabinet when I realized that I didn't know the name of the secretary of agriculture. Not only that: I realized that nobody knows the name of the secretary of agriculture — a fact that severely limits the impact of speculating about what sort of intimate decoration he might be sporting on his seat.

I cheered myself with the thought that I wouldn't have wanted to take the standard approach anyway. I could begin instead with the theory that Shultz's people, fearful that he was getting a reputation for being a stolid and unimaginative clod, themselves floated the rumor that in his wild youth at Princeton he had the team mascot tattooed on his posterior — a little disinformation, you might say. Of course, the fact that a tiger tattoo was their idea of dash raises the possibility that they are themselves stolid and unimaginative clods, but that might be material for another column.

"The reason that poor Shultz is getting the reputation of a dull plodder — and this will be the heart of the column — is that the right-wing wackos around the Administration keep going behind his back and accusing him of overt sanity," I told my wife, as I more or less began to talk out the rough draft.

"I think you've used that before," she said.

"Used what before?"

"Used that business about how people in this Administration suffer politically from suspicions of sanity," she said. "As I remember, you mentioned a newspaper story about some deputy attorney general's 'pragmatism' that you said should actually have been headlined TOP JUSTICE AIDE WIDELY CONSIDERED NOT LOONY."

"Well," I said. "I'm grateful that you've been reading the columns so closely. I think."

That wasn't my only approach, of course. It had occurred to me, for instance, that if this sort of thing caught on, all sorts of kinky rumors would be floated by staff people — particularly about those Cabinet members who can't seem to get into the newspapers any other way. "I can see an item surfacing in one of the columns about how Otis R. Bowen, the secretary of Health and Human Services, used to enter tango contests," I said to my wife. "The next thing you know, the people over at the Department of Energy have leaked a rumor that the secretary there, John S. Herrington, makes it a custom to celebrate every Groundhog Day by costuming as Catherine of Aragon."

"But you can't write that sort of thing," my wife said. "People will sue."

"I don't think a public figure can sue," I said.

"A public figure who is accused of walking around in a Catherine of Aragon costume can sue," she said.

I really hadn't thought of that. I could use another approach, of course, but one didn't come to mind right off hand. Just then the telephone rang. It was my old Army buddy Charlie, showing the first interest he had ever exhibited in my column.

"I can't wait to read what you say about Shultz having a tiger tattooed on his rear," Charlie said. "What a hoot!"

"I'm not actually going to be writing about that, Charlie," I said. "I like to think I'm above that sort of thing."

Managing the Cherry Tree Scandal

February 2, 1987

"O.K., THE WAY I SEE IT is that we've got to have him say something about the cherry tree business. Let's get it out and get it behind him."

"I say we stonewall. He doesn't mention the cherry tree. At all. Ever. Sooner or later, his old man is going to forget about it."

"Josiah, the cherry tree is lying there on the ground. George's old man could come home any night and trip on it. Right, George? . . . George? George, could you please pay a little attention? We're trying to help you, George."

"And you're doing a great job. This is the greatest collection of colonies in the history of the world because of people just like you: the Carolina planter developing great plantations with very little attrition in the slave supply, the Massachusetts entrepreneur snookering the Indians out of most of New England, the learned speech-writers and colonial spin-merchants right here trying to help a young boy such as myself get by this little mix-up with the cherry —"

"Fine, George. Great stuff. As I was saying, gentlemen, let's play to George's strength: he tells a fantastic story. Look how he put across that business about throwing a silver dollar across the Rappahannock."

"I'll admit he was terrific with that one — the way he looked right straight at that crowd down at the feed store and said, 'I threw a silver dollar across the Rappahannock, and if we get the King's tax collectors off our backs everyone can throw a silver dollar across the Rappahannock, and soon the deficit will simply disappear.'"

"You mean I didn't really throw a silver dollar across the Rappahannock?"

"Of course you did, George. Great toss, guy!"

"Sure you did, George. You were marvelous. George, maybe you could just go back to staring out the window for a while until we've worked this thing out."

"Look, George's old man isn't going to fall again for that song and dance about the orchard being attacked by a pack of mad beavers."

"Actually, I thought George carried that off pretty well. It was certainly better than the time the old man demanded to know what happened to a cherry tree and George said, 'What cherry tree?'"

"You mean I've chopped down cherry trees before?"

"Oh, no, George. I don't know what gave you that idea."

"No indeed, George. You're a fine citizen."

"Yes, citizens all: the Pennsylvania forge-owner importing fine little bond servants from English debtors' prisons, the Connecticut land speculator . . ."

"That's great, George. But why don't you just hold on there for a minute, and we'll let you know when we get this thing sorted out."

"I still say we have George walk right up to his father, say 'I chopped down the cherry tree,' ask the old guy's forgiveness, and then try to get on with his legendary childhood. Maybe we can set up an oil-painting opportunity with George pretending to fling a silver dollar across the Rappahannock."

"No, I say we go back to the story we had at the start: mistakes were made and the kid down the road made them."

"That story's got problems, Jedediah. First off, the kid down the road doesn't have an ax. Also, the kid down the road happens to be a slave and happens to belong to George, even if George does have a little trouble remembering his name."

"Well then, George tells the old man that he's going to get to the bottom of this as soon as he remembers the kid down the road's name."

"Or maybe he says, 'Father, I know we share the goal of fine cherries, and I took the risk that chopping down the tree would help us attain that goal, and I'd take such a risk again except that we don't have any cherry trees left.'"

"No. No. George should take the responsibility, because the old man already knows that George is in charge of the orchard — and that way he won't get the blame, because the old man also knows that George probably can't tell a cherry tree from a large pile of crabgrass."

"He should just say, 'I chopped down the cherry tree, and I ask you to trust me anyway because I have never chopped down a cherry tree before, and also I once threw a silver dollar across the Rappahannock."

"No, no, no, no, no. You never use the first person in these things, and you never use the active voice. If George has to say anything, he should say, 'Father, I cannot tell a lie: a cherry tree was chopped down.'"

". . . yes, those are the people who have made these colonies great: the Virginia cherry-grower thinning out his orchards, the New England whaler courageously killing off . . ."

"I still say we stonewall."

Chances Are

February 9, 1987

I SAW A PROFESSOR of business on television saying that there's a new millionaire in the United States every thirty-nine minutes. So I waited. Nothing happened. I don't mean the world stood still; for instance, the show with the professor on it ended and female wrestling from Japan came on. What I mean is that I didn't become a millionaire. I asked my wife if she thought my watch might be running fast. Maybe thirty-nine minutes hadn't actually elapsed. My wife said it didn't have anything to do with my watch. I figured she was probably right, but I waited a couple of minutes just in case. Nothing happened.

My wife said that I have no grasp of the mathematical principles underlying statistics and probabilities — which sounds bad but, I have to admit, is not the worst thing she's ever said about me. Then she started to laugh.

"If you're laughing at the female wrestling from Japan," I said, "I think I should tell you that the name Freight Train Yagamora does not sound in the least

humorous to a Japanese person. The same is true of
Whole Hog Nakaguru. Also, taking a person by the hair
and beating her head against the ring-post may have a
ritualistic significance in Japan that is quite serious, particularly for the person whose head it is."

"That's not why I'm laughing," she said. "I'm laughing
because you think you can become a millionaire by sitting
here watching female wrestling from Japan."

"The way I understood the professor, what a person's
watching wouldn't affect the odds," I told her. "Now that
you mention it, though, it might have been a good idea
to watch *Masterpiece Theatre*, so that when I became
a millionaire I'd become a cultured millionaire."

"Where did you think the money was going to come
from?" she asked.

"I really hadn't given it that much thought," I said.
"I've been pretty busy here, you know, checking my
watch constantly and just glancing over at the TV now
and then when something exciting happened. Actually,
when the referee was trying to keep Whole Hog Nakaguru from jumping up and down on Freight Train
Yagamora's nose, I got so engrossed I pretty much lost
track of time."

Reminded of the match, I glanced over just then to see
Whole Hog jumping up and down on the referee's nose.
When she had finished, I turned to my wife and said, "I
suppose it might have come from something like a lottery
— something that doesn't take much time and doesn't
require leaving the room."

In fact, people who are doing nothing more remarkable
than watching wrestling on TV win the lottery all the
time. As it happens, my own brother-in-law won the

Missouri state lottery. It's true that he won only a hundred thousand dollars instead of a million, but maybe he didn't wait the full thirty-nine minutes.

"You've never bought a lottery ticket," my wife said.

I hate it when she says things like that. I know she means well, but I just think you can carry this mathematical-probabilities business too far. Last summer, for instance, we took a trip to Europe around the time the airline industry was trying to reassure tourists by telling them that their chances of becoming the victim of an act of terrorism were less than their chances of drowning in the bathtub, and I said I felt particularly secure because I only take showers. My wife said that was a misunderstanding of the mathematical principle involved, and I felt jumpy for the rest of the summer.

My wife started laughing again. I thought she saw something funny in the fact that both Whole Hog Nakaguru and the referee had just landed in the sixth row, but then she said, "I just remembered the time we saw that television interview with the publisher who was bragging so much about the improvements he had made in his magazine's demographics. When he said that he had managed to lower the age of the average subscriber by three years, you said maybe we ought to get Uncle Harry a subscription because he might be easier for Aunt Rosie to take if he were sixty-eight instead of seventy-one."

"Well, Aunt Rosie thought it was worth a shot," I said.

I was becoming a bit concerned about Whole Hog, who hadn't emerged from beneath the seats, but my wife burst out laughing again. When she was able to get her breath well enough to talk, she said, "How would you calculate the odds of winning the lottery for someone who hasn't bought a ticket?"

"It's too late anyway," I said, looking at my watch. "Forty-six minutes have passed. That professor must have been dead wrong."

Gentlemanly Acts

February 16, 1987

A FRIEND I'LL CALL Bill Smith is often complimented on his gentlemanly comportment. You don't often hear people complimented for manners of any sort these days. Just to give you an example, I've almost never heard myself complimented on my gentlemanly comportment. In fact, it has been so long since anyone remarked on my gentlemanliness — I was ten, and I had just held a door for my Aunt Rosie — that, had we been living in a more mannerly age, I might have had to consider the possibility that people have come to think of me as a crude and graceless oaf.

No fear of that, of course, since we do not live in a time when manners are given high priority. In fact, there was a period several years ago when militant feminists let it be known that they despised traditional gentlemanly gestures as symbols of the old pedestal days — meaning that men like my old Army buddy Charlie, who had previously been considered hopeless slobs, could think of themselves instead as sufficiently liberated to have no use for the customs of the oppressor-male.

That period seems to have ended; a distinguished classics professor of old-fashioned habits can now open a door for a female graduate student without much fear that he'll get a nasty remark or a karate chop for his trouble. Charlie is back to being considered gross beyond measure, and Bill Smith is getting more compliments than ever on his gentlemanly ways.

Smith, who lives in Greenwich Village now, comes from California, which is not noted for excessive courtliness. He has worked most of his life in journalism, a field that, I must admit, may have more than its share of crude and graceless oafs. I asked him once how he accounted for his manners, and he unhesitantly gave all credit to a series of lectures all boys in his junior high school were required to attend on the subject of Gentlemanly Comportment. Although Smith was in junior high school back in the forties, he assured me that he still remembers everything he learned in Gentlemanly Comportment — a particularly remarkable statement when you stop to consider how much math has slipped away from him during the same period.

Smith even remembers who gave the lectures — a vice principal who spent the summer months working for the Park Service in one of the nearby national parks and is always referred to by Smith as Ranger-Naturalist Floyd Brown. Although Smith assures me that during the school year Ranger-Naturalist Floyd Brown wore the sort of clothes normally associated with junior high school administrators — a chalky suit, I suppose — I have always envisioned him presenting his Gentlemanly Comportment lectures in his full ranger-naturalist uniform, including a broad-brimmed Smokey the Bear hat. He stands there, almost at attention, and just when you think he's about to tell you the difference between a juniper and a common grass snake, he starts talking about the absolute necessity of a gentleman's rising when a lady enters the room.

For all Smith knows, Ranger-Naturalist Floyd Brown might have been fuzzy on juniper identification, but he had definite opinions when it came to manners. For instance, he believed that a gentleman who was crossing the street with a lady always — no exceptions — walked between the lady and the approaching traffic. I pointed out to Smith that, assuming the street being crossed has traffic in both directions, that rule requires a sudden switch in the middle of the street.

"Absolutely," Smith said. "In fact, Ranger-Naturalist Floyd Brown always made that point by asking a question that he answered himself. 'Does the rule mean that you must change sides in the middle of the street?' he'd ask. 'Yes, it does.' "

Smith told me that even now, many years after the Gentlemanly Comportment course, he still follows the rules of Ranger-Naturalist Floyd Brown to the letter. It struck me as odd that a tourist in Greenwich Village who saw someone suddenly jump to the other side of his partner while crossing the street might think he was witnessing yet another demonstration of bizarre Village behavior when, in fact, he was seeing Bill Smith follow the rules of Gentlemanly Comportment as laid down by Ranger-Naturalist Floyd Brown in Glendale, California, in 1948.

When I said that to Smith, he pointed out that the Village is almost entirely one-way streets, but that he still gets to show his stuff when he and his wife, taking a stroll uptown, have reason to cross Forty-second Street or Central Park West.

"But what does she say when you suddenly leap to the other side of her in the middle of the street?" I asked.

Smith smiled. "Often," he said, "she compliments me on my gentlemanly comportment."

Flunking the Bank Exam

February 23, 1987

MY BANK ASKED ME to leave. I know what you're thinking. Simply because I'm known as someone who displays some impatience with the new technology now and then, you're thinking that I probably got into a shouting match with an automatic teller machine. You think I stood there shouting personal insults ("I've seen better screens than yours on the windows of chicken coops!") and invoking curses ("May your chips fall where they may!"), the machine replied insultingly in its irritating beepspeak, and a bank guard finally came over to me and said, "I'm afraid I'll have to ask you to leave, sir. You're disturbing the other machines."

That's not the way it happened at all. Just to show you how wrong you are, my bank is too fancy to have automatic teller machines. This is the sort of bank that has thick carpets and marble pillars. Even its name is fancy: Morgan Guaranty Trust. I know what you're wondering. You're wondering why such a fancy bank would have a customer like me.

Here's how it happened. A company I went to work for had many millions of dollars moldering away at the Morgan Guaranty Trust, and its employees were therefore given free Morgan Guaranty checking accounts. For years and years, we banked at the Morgan Guaranty, treading with pleasure on the thick carpets and rubbing up against the smooth marble pillars, and nobody could tell us from the people who belonged there.

Then we all got notices from the Morgan saying that it was going to start charging monthly fees — rather high monthly fees — for our checking accounts. I assumed that the owners of our company, faced with this affront to their loyal employees, would threaten to let the moldering millions molder away elsewhere if the Morgan didn't change its tune — and might even pound on one of the Morgan's highly polished tables during the discussion in a way that left fingerprints, just as a hint of the backup muscle available. Not exactly. What the owners of our company said was, "Well, O.K."

As we approached the date when monthly charges for checking accounts would begin, all of our people snatched up their money and left for less fancy banks, gazing back longingly at the marble pillars and thick carpets. Except me. The date had slipped my mind. The next month, though, I noticed that there was no charge for my checking account. Maybe they'd been bluffing. I waited another month, risking what I figured would be at least seven dollars for the first month's fee if I turned out to be wrong. No charge. Months followed with no charge. Then years. Now that I was about the only one from my company left at the Morgan, it was harder than ever to tell me from the people who belonged there. After a while, even I had trouble telling me from the people who belonged there.

Then I got another notice about the bank's having found it necessary to institute monthly charges on all checking acccounts. I ignored it. On purpose. No charge. More years passed. They were free years.

I had more than a free checking account at a fancy bank. I had something to talk about whenever I ran into my old college acquaintance, Martin G. Kashfleau, the Wall Street operator who was in the habit of asking me what I'd been up to and then looking disappointed when I didn't report that I had just done some deals with what he always calls "major players."

"I've just called the Morgan's bluff on a couple of deals," I'd say to Kashfleau. "I decided to show them how hardball is played."

Then, this fall, I got a notice saying that for checking accounts under ten thousand dollars — which, I regret to say, is an exceedingly discreet description of my checking account — there would henceforth be a quarterly charge of $250. They might be bluffing again, but it could cost me $250 to find out.

"I suppose they don't know who they're dealing with," I said to my wife.

"Or they do," my wife said.

"It's the equivalent of asking me to leave," I said. "Well, I know when I'm not wanted. I shall take my funds elsewhere."

On the day I left the Morgan, taking one last little hop on the thick carpet as I approached the door, my wife thought I needed some cheering — maybe because I occasionally turned to strangers in the subway and said, "My bank has asked me to leave." She reminded me that my new bank would at least have automatic teller machines. She was right. The first day, I got into an argument with one. When I gave it a little kick, a bank guard looked in my direction, but I wasn't worried. "Take it easy," I'd say. "I've been asked to leave fancier banks than this."

Tokyo Law

March 2, 1987

JUST WHEN I THOUGHT there was no way to stop the Japanese from steadily widening their lead over American industry, I saw a headline in the paper that said JAPAN TO OPEN ITS DOORS TO AMERICAN LAWYERS. That ought to do it.

I don't know which deputy undersecretary of what talked the Japanese into allowing American lawyers to practice over there, but whoever it was should be made secretary of state tomorrow. The Japanese had to have been aware of the sheer number of lawyers in America. According to statistics I saw a few years ago, American law schools turn out as many lawyers every year as there are lawyers in Japan altogether. We're producing that many new ones annually on top of what is already, to put it as nicely as I can manage, a surplus. As any lawyer specializing in international trade could tell you, if you happened to be willing to pay him $250 an hour plus expenses, those are the classic conditions that lead to dumping.

I suspect our guy softened up the Japanese by flooding Japanese television with old *Perry Mason* reruns, so that they'd think American lawyers are serious men who, without giving much thought to their own fee, save innocent people from jail in the five minutes between the soy sauce commercial and the end of the show. Then, somehow, he suckered them into opening the doors.

I realize that the headline writer was simply using a metaphor, but when I read that phrase about the doors I couldn't help envisioning a real door being opened. That response might have had something to do with my childhood: whenever my mother left us kids alone in the house, her parting words were, "Remember, don't open the door to any lawyers."

As I see it, the man who hears the knock is a small, exceedingly polite Japanese gentleman named Mr. Yamaguto — the chief executive officer of Kondetzu, a company so much more efficient than its American counterparts that it has a lock on contracts to provide eighty percent of the U.S. Army's tanks, the auditorium sound system for the Miss America contest, and the official baseball for both major leagues. Mr. Yamaguto smiles as he goes to the door. He is expecting Perry Mason. He's thinking that Perry Mason just might have brought along that nice secretary of his. He opens the door. He bows. Twenty-six thousand American lawyers walk in.

Within a month, fourteen thousand of them are billing Kondetzu for legal services, at rates that range from $200 to $350 an hour. Legal expenses have forced the company to put off a retooling of its food-service division, and, for the first time in ten years, it has lost the annual contract awarded for the supplying of apple pies to American Legion halls. Mr. Yamaguto has less and less time for management of the company, since he is often meeting with his lawyers or trying to figure out how to pay lawyers or defending himself from the lawyers hired by dissatisfied employees and dissident stockholders or giving depositions to lawyers in the negligence case several lawyers persuaded him to bring after he was bowled over at the door-opening and suffered what they call "potential psychoneurotic whiplash."

All over Japan, other small, exceedingly polite gentlemen have opened doors only to be trampled by hordes of American lawyers, and billed for it. American imports increase as Japanese industry begins to sag under the weight of legal advice. Within a couple of years, Tokyo teenagers are walking around plugged into a version of the Walkman manufactured in Gary, Indiana. An American company now has the contract to provide replacement cars for the bullet train between Tokyo and Kyoto. No master sushi chef in Japan will work without a contract guaranteeing him an adequate supply of American knives — a contract hammered out by huge teams of American lawyers on both sides. Within five years, the economy of the Japanese is in such bad shape that you'd think they were the ones who lost the Second World War.

By that time, the way I figure it, the genius who negotiated this deal has been sent off to undermine some of our other competitors. American conglomerateurs and corporate raiders have been allowed into West Germany, and BMWs are beginning to come off the line with engine knocks and missing fenders as management increasingly turns its attention to staving off a takeover bid by a company whose main line of work is the manufacture of frozen bratwurst dinners. Finally, with the dollar strong and Midwestern assembly lines humming, there is a headline that reflects the great negotiator's most spectacular triumph: SOVIET UNION TO OPEN ITS DOORS TO AMERICAN LIFE INSURANCE SALESMEN.

Inspecting the Cork

March 16, 1987

THIS SUPPOSEDLY TOOK PLACE at a particularly fancy restaurant somewhere in the United States — the sort of restaurant I've always referred to as La Maison de la Casa House, Continental Cuisine. The wine waiter — or the sommelier, as the folks at La Maison de la Casa House would certainly have called him — arrived at the table with the expensive bottle of wine that had just been ordered. He displayed the label, opened the bottle, placed the cork on the table in front of the customer who had done the ordering, and poured an inch or so of wine to be tasted. The customer ignored the wine in his glass, but he ate the cork.

I came across the story in a recent speech about the trials facing someone trying to serve wine to the sort of untutored clods who frequent American restaurants — a speech that had the tone of those nineteenth-century accounts of the frustrations experienced by someone trying to bring a working knowledge of Latin grammar to the Hottentots.

It was obvious to me that the story-teller didn't understand the story he was telling. He assumed that the cork was eaten out of ignorance. He didn't realize that there are any number of Americans who might want to eat a cork for effect. In other words, we are dealing here with someone who never met my old Army buddy Charlie.

I could easily imagine Charlie eating a cork — although I'll admit that it takes a leap of imagination to envision him in a fancy restaurant, particularly if he happened to be wearing his Jayhawk sweatshirt. I've mentioned Charlie's sweatshirt before. It's bright red, and it's designed to look like a jayhawk, beginning with two huge eyes around chest level. Charlie wears it as a symbol of the semester and a half he put in at the University of Kansas before what he always refers to as "the little trouble down at the Tri-Delt house." I don't think cork-eating would present any physical problems that Charlie couldn't handle: he always used to delight in startling convenience-store clerks by finishing off a bag of Fritos in four or five bites without opening it. All in all, I think Charlie would consider cork-eating what he sometimes refers to as "a real hoot."

I can envision any number of ways he might do it. He might swallow the whole thing at once — an alternative available to someone who has always been able to put his gullet on automatic pilot and pour down a couple of cans of Schlitz — or he might put it in his mouth and wash it down with water, as if it were a particularly large anti-cold tablet he had been instructed to take immediately before meals. He might take a small bite, spit it onto the floor, and shout, "You call that cork, my man!" Or he might finish up the cork, turn to the rest of the people at the table, and say, "I'm not a doctor, but I play one on TV, so I know the importance of fiber in your diet . . ."

I think it's more likely, though, that he'd raise the cork to his mouth and chomp off a big bite, as if he were eating a radish. I can just see him chewing the bite slowly, staring very hard at the sommelier the entire time, and doing that trick he does with his stomach to make the beak of the jayhawk seem to open and close. The rest of the people in Charlie's party — the band of galoots Charlie often introduces as "my good friends and accessories" — are playing along, of course. They continue their small talk, occasionally glancing over at Charlie to see if he seems to be satisfied with what he's eating. Maybe a couple of them try to get the sommelier's attention so that they can ask him whether he would recommend a red or a white for chug-a-lugging.

The sommelier is trying to muster the polite and expectant expression he learned in sommelier school, but his face is drained of color and he is emitting some soft beeping sounds that might be sighs or groans. The proprietor, who has come over to see what's going on, at first stands there with a fixed smile. Then he begins to look desperate as he notices other diners following Charlie's example. All over the restaurant, diners are eating their corks. Then Charlie finally swallows what he has been chewing, puts the rest of the cork back on the table, pauses for a moment to give the matter one last bit of consideration, and turns to the sommelier. "Fine," Charlie says. "That's fine. It's not the year I ordered, but it's fine."

Success

March 9, 1987

A YOUNG MAN of humble origins came to New York from the Midwest to seek his fortune. He dreamed, in the American way, of becoming a millionaire. He tried his luck on Wall Street. He was diligent and shrewd and, when he had to be, devious. He put together the National Worldwide Universal deal and he did some things with an electronics acquisition that wouldn't bear explaining. He succeeded even beyond his dream: he made twelve million dollars.

At first the young man assumed that everything was working out splendidly. "Isn't it grand?" he said to his wife, once it was apparent that he had made twelve million dollars.

"No, it isn't," his wife said. "You're a nobody."

"But that's impossible," the young man said. "I'm a rich person. We live in an era that celebrates rich people. Rich people are shown in the newspapers in the company of movie stars and famous novelists and distinguished dress designers. The names of the richest corporate raiders are known to every schoolboy. There are rich real estate sharks whose faces appear on the covers of glossy magazines."

"Yours won't," his wife said. "You're a nobody."

"But I have twelve million dollars," the young man said.

"So do a lot of people," his wife said. "They're nobodies, too."

"I could buy our way onto the committees of important charity balls," the young man said. "Then we'd be mentioned in the columns."

"Don't kid yourself," his wife said. "The important committees are already filled up with people who are really rich. People like us would end up working on something like a dinner-dance to benefit the American Psoriasis Foundation."

"But I own a co-op apartment on Fifth Avenue that's worth two million dollars," the young man said.

"Two-million-dollar co-ops are a dime a dozen," his wife said. "So to speak."

"I have a stretch limousine," the young man said. "It's twenty-one and a half feet long."

"Nobody famous has ever ridden in it," his wife said. "Henry Kissinger and Calvin Klein have never heard of you. You're a nobody."

The young man was silent for a while. "Are you disappointed in me?" he finally said to his wife.

"Of course I'm disappointed in you," she said. "When you asked me to marry you, you said you would surely amount to something. How was I to know that you'd turn out to be a nobody?"

For a moment the young man looked defeated. Then he squared his shoulders and cleared his throat. "I'll make them pay attention," he said. "I'll buy a professional football team and argue a lot with the coach in public. Celebrities will join me to watch big games from the owner's box."

"You can't buy a professional football team for twelve million dollars," his wife said. "Professional football teams cost big bucks."

"Then I'll buy a magazine and appoint myself chief columnist," the young man said. "A tiny but exceedingly flattering picture of me will run next to my column every week. The owners of professional football teams will invite me to watch big games from the owner's box."

"You might be able to buy one of those weekly-shopper throwaways for twelve million dollars, but not a real magazine," his wife said. "You can't buy a real magazine for chicken feed."

"Is that what you call what we have?" the young man asked. "Is twelve million dollars chicken feed?"

"It's not big bucks," his wife said. "What can I tell you?"

"But that's not fair," the young man said. "I'm a young man of humble origins who made twelve million dollars. I succeeded even beyond my dream."

"Some of those things you did with the electronics acquisition probably weren't fair either," his wife said. "Fair isn't being measured these days. What they measure is money."

"Then I'll get more money," the young man said. "I'm going to go back to Wall Street and make fifty million dollars."

But before the young man could make fifty million dollars a man from the Securities and Exchange Commission came and arrested him for having committed insider-trading violations in the electronics acquisition.

The young man was taken away from his office in hand-cuffs. A picture on the front page of the afternoon paper showed him leaving his arraignment, trying to hide his face behind an $850 Italian overcoat. A long article in the morning paper used him as an example of a new breed of Wall Street traders who were the victims of their own greed, probably because of their humble origins. His friends and associates avoided him.

Only his wife stuck by him. She tried to see the bright side. "For someone with only twelve million dollars," she said to the young man, "you're getting to be pretty well known."